Philippa Foot's Moral Thought

Philippa Foot's Moral Thought

JOHN HACKER-WRIGHT

BLOOMSBURY

LONDON • NEW DELHI • NEW YORK • SYDNEY

Bloomsbury Academic

An imprint of Bloomsbury Publishing Plc

50 Bedford Square
London
WC1B 3DP
UK

1385 Broadway
New York
NY 10018
USA

www.bloomsbury.com

First published 2013

© John Hacker-Wright, 2013

British Library Cataloguing-in-Publication Data
A catalogue record for this book is available from the British Library.

ISBN: HB: 978-1-4411-0410-6
PB: 978-1-4411-9184-7
ePub: 978-1-4411-5738-6
ePDF: 978-1-4411-8668-3

Library of Congress Cataloging-in-Publication Data
Hacker-Wright, John.
Philippa Foot's moral thought/John Hacker-Wright.
pages cm
Includes bibliographical references and index.
ISBN 978-1-4411-9184-7 (pbk.) – ISBN 978-1-4411-0410-6 –
ISBN 978-1-4411-5738-6 (epub) – ISBN 978-1-4411-8668-3 (pdf)
1. Foot, Philippa. I. Title.
BJ604.F663H33 2013
170.92–dc23
2013005644

Typeset by Deanta Global Publishing Services, Chennai, India
Printed and bound in India

For Nigel and Blaise

CONTENTS

ACKNOWLEDGMENTS

This book was prepared with financial support from the Canada's Social Sciences and Humanities Research Council. I would like to thank Kyle Bromhall, John Law, and Brian Rogers for research and editorial assistance. Debra Lawson carefully edited the manuscript and made a number of helpful suggestions. Erin Flynn made numerous suggestions on Chapter 7. Discussions with Richard Hamilton, Rosalind Hursthouse, and Peter Loptson have helped with the development of many of the ideas here. Above all, thanks to Laura Hacker-Wright for support through the writing process.

ABBREVIATIONS

Works by Philippa Foot

MD   *Moral Dilemmas and Other Topics in Moral Philosophy.* Oxford: Oxford University Press, 2002.

NG   *Natural Goodness.* Oxford: Oxford University Press, 2001.

PDM   "The Philosopher's Defence of Morality." *Philosophy* 27, no. 103 (1952): 311–28.

RG   "Rationality and Goodness" in O'Hear, Anthony, ed. *Modern Moral Philosophy: Royal Institute of Philosophy Supplement: 54.* Cambridge: Cambridge University Press, 2004.

TE   Introduction to *Theories of Ethics.* Oxford: Oxford University Press, 1976.

VV   *Virtues and Vices and Other Essays in Moral Philosophy,* 2nd edn. Oxford: Oxford University Press, 2002.

WPMP   "When Is a Principle a Moral Principle?" *Aristotelian Society Supplementary Volume* 28 (1954): 95–110.

Introduction

In introductory ethics courses, Adolf Hitler often appears as a figure that both teachers and students can agree on—he is evil. In such contexts, he serves as a very convenient figure since we can be sure of not offending anyone by placing him in such a category. Yet, these frequent references to Hitler and the Nazis may inure us to the gravity of the issue that is raised by our evident disagreement with them. After all, is there any way to confirm that our judgments are correct, and that Hitler and his followers are indeed wrong? Or is this merely a gut-level reaction that has no further defense? Philippa Foot's career in philosophy is motivated by questions arising from the historical context of the horrific acts that Hitler and his regime perpetrated against the European Jews. In an interview published initially in 2003, Foot said:

> I was always interested in philosophy. But it was significant that the news of the concentration camps hit us just when I came back to Oxford in 1945. This news was shattering in a fashion that no one now can easily understand. We had thought that something like this could not happen. This is what got me interested in moral philosophy in particular.[1]

Foot's interest in moral philosophy emerged when something she thought morally impossible actually occurred. This unsettling experience eventually led her to challenge one of the prevailing orthodoxies in moral philosophy at that time—two rational people may agree about all the facts and yet still arrive at conflicting moral judgments. According to the views Foot ultimately rejected, morality is essentially a matter of one's attitudes toward a set of facts, and it is possible for two rational people to have opposed attitudes toward the same facts. In regard to the Nazis, we can easily see that there were, in fact, two irreconcilable attitudes toward eradicating the European Jews—that of a Nazi true believer, who approves of it, and that of the right thinking non-Nazi, who disapproves of it. These two groups, then, may have agreed on all of the facts, and yet they still came to very different moral conclusions.[2] But are they both correct? And are they both rational?

On the prevailing view, known as noncognitivism, there simply is no matter of correctness since moral judgments are a matter of attitude. My assessment that the non-Nazis are "right thinking" reflects my attitude of approval toward them, and if I am tempted to say that the Nazis are incorrect in their moral judgments, this view expresses my condemnation of them. According to noncognitivism, both parties could also be fully rational. Let us suppose that they fully register all of the relevant facts; in acting on their opposed moral attitudes, they may each be rational because, in so acting, they are presumably fulfilling desires that correspond to their various attitudes. Of course, many other attitudes and desires may come into play in determining the practical rationality of acting on their moral judgments. Still, it is by recourse to the desires of the agent that the question of whether a given action is rational is to be decided.

Throughout her philosophical career, Foot consistently answers "no" to the first question—in her view, the Nazis are clearly wrong and their opponents are correct in their condemnation of them. In writings from the late 1950s through to her final work in 2004, Foot held that there are facts that must be taken into account in arriving at a moral judgment, and it is possible to be wrong in our moral judgments in much the same sense as it is possible to be wrong about whether it is raining outside. This view is compatible with saying that both parties to a dispute are rational in acting on their opposed judgments. For instance, one might say that the Nazis are incorrect in their moral judgments, but rational nonetheless. In fact, this is a position that Foot takes at one point in her philosophical career, although she comes to adopt the view that the Nazis (and anyone else who acts immorally) are both incorrect and irrational. Foot is notorious for arguing that perhaps the Nazis (or any other immoral agent) can be rational in ignoring morality. Yet, in so arguing, she was adhering to what many philosophers already thought about practical rationality, namely, that it was a matter of maximizing the fulfillment of our desires or, in some cases, acting in our interests. In other writings, including her last works, Foot rejects this view of how morality provides us with reasons in favor of one in which morality gives us reasons to act in accordance with it, regardless of our desires.

We see, then, two central preoccupations of Foot's philosophical career—the nature of morality and how morality provides us with reasons to act. A third question she addresses is—which actions are morally right? This question concerns the content of morality, which Foot addressed in application to controversial issues such as abortion and euthanasia. Nearly all of her relatively small body of work falls within these three areas. Though Foot is a clear writer and thinker, her work is lapidary and dense with argumentation, which makes it difficult to approach, especially for a reader not immersed in the context of the debates she addresses. The task of this critical survey of Foot's philosophy is to help such a reader access Foot's thought and to provide a guide for its continuing relevance within current philosophy.

An intellectual biographical sketch

Philippa Foot was born Philippa Judith Bosanquet on October 3, 1920, in Owston Ferry, Lincolnshire, and grew up in Kirkleatham in North Yorkshire, England. Her mother, Esther, was the daughter of U.S. President Grover Cleveland. Her father, William, was an industrialist, running a large Yorkshire steel works. Foot studied philosophy, politics, and economics at Somerville College, a women's college within the University of Oxford. Foot had no formal education as a child; as she puts it, she "lived in the sort of milieu where there was a lot of hunting, shooting, and fishing, and where girls simply did not go to college."[3] In her youth, she was educated by governesses, from whom she claimed she did not even learn "which came first, the Romans or the Greeks."[4]

Her earliest philosophy tutor at Somerville was Donald MacKinnon, a philosopher and theologian with an interest in Plotinus, Kant, and Hegel. Foot earned a BLitt from Somerville for her research on Kant, and followed this graduate bachelor's degree by holding a fellowship at her alma mater. Foot credits her introduction to analytic philosophy to G. E. M. Anscombe, a leading analytic philosopher who made significant contributions to ethics, philosophy of action, and metaphysics; Anscombe was also Foot's colleague at Somerville. She reports that they would talk over philosophical issues daily after lunch and attend each other's seminars. At the time, they disagreed on many issues, and Foot found herself regularly defeated in arguments with Anscombe. She describes the experience as if she were a character in a children's comic "who becomes flattened – an outline on the ground – but the character is there in the next episode unscathed."[5]

As we will see in the course of this book, Anscombe was a highly significant influence on Foot. Her early work draws on Anscombe's philosophy of action, and the two shared a conviction that the virtues were more significant for moral philosophy than they had been taken to be by their peers. Anscombe also imparted an appreciation for the philosophy of Thomas Aquinas, upon whom Foot draws extensively in the development of her theory of virtue and its role in morality.

Another influence on Foot was the philosopher and novelist Iris Murdoch, the dedicatee of Foot's first collection of essays, *Virtues and Vices*. The two were flat mates in London during the war, after their graduation from Somerville, and their friendship continued despite the fact that after Murdoch and her husband M. R. D. Foot divorced, Philippa subsequently married him. Foot does not make explicit reference to Murdoch's published work; yet, Murdoch's philosophy also focused on the importance of the virtues for moral philosophy.

Foot began lecturing in philosophy at Somerville in 1947. In 1974, she took up a position at the University of California, Los Angeles (UCLA), where she remained until retirement in 1991. One of the most important influences on her later philosophical work was a colleague at UCLA, Warren Quinn. They shared a nonconsequentialist moral outlook; Quinn's work on rationality was especially important to Foot's second change of mind on the issue of how morality furnishes us with reasons for action. Another major influence on Foot's later work was her student Michael Thompson, now professor of philosophy at the University of Pittsburgh; his work helped Foot to formulate her final ethical naturalism, as defended in her 2001 book, *Natural Goodness*. Foot's last philosophical article appeared in 2004, and she died on her ninetieth birthday—October 3, 2010.

Foot's philosophical career lends itself to division between early, middle, and late periods, as her student Gavin Lawrence has pointed out (VR 89). In her early work, she defends the objectivity of moral norms, demonstrating their essential connection to facts about what is good for human beings. Also, in this early period's work, she defends moral rationalism, which is the idea that morality gives reasons for action to everyone, even those who lack the desire to do what is right. In her middle period, she changes her mind on this issue and attacks moral rationalism in one of her most celebrated articles, "Morality as a System of Hypothetical Imperatives." In this period, she also turns to writing on controversial moral issues such as abortion and euthanasia. Finally, in her late period, she reverses her thoughts again on moral rationalism and adopts a different view on the nature of rationality—rather than undertake to establish that moral behavior is rational by a morally neutral standard of rationality, such as the fulfillment of our desires, she argues that morality ought to be thought of as part of the standard of rationality itself. Also, in this last phase of her work, she offers a view of the relationship of morality to human nature, arguing that the moral virtues are part of what makes us good as human beings.

Outline of the book

This book follows the development of Foot's moral philosophy in a roughly chronological fashion. Chapter 1 treats the context of Foot's early contributions to moral philosophy, tracing the history of moral philosophy from G. E. Moore to R. M. Hare. Readers who are unfamiliar with this history will want to start here, as grasping Foot's moral philosophy depends on a thorough understanding of this philosophical background.

Chapter 2 focuses on Foot's early arguments against R. M. Hare's prescriptivism in favor of a form of ethical naturalism, which is the view that moral judgments are grounded in appeal to facts about the world. In this chapter, I consider her arguments in favor of our ability to derive evaluative judgments from factual judgments. The success of these arguments is still in question, but I make a case for slightly amended versions of those arguments. Also in this chapter, I discuss her early arguments in favor of moral rationalism. Although

Foot ends up abandoning the position that she advocates here, it is unclear whether she is correct in doing so. I make a case for this view.

Chapter 3 focuses entirely on Foot's notorious article, "Morality as a System of Hypothetical Imperatives." This single work inspired a vast philosophical literature on the nature of moral reasons. I situate Foot's article within this literature and, ultimately, argue against Foot's middle period view, but point out some common misunderstandings of that view along the way.

Chapter 4 treats Foot's views on the virtues in depth. She is often thought of as a virtue ethicist but, though her work is clearly a touchstone for contemporary virtue ethics, she explicitly disavows that her moral philosophy should be thought of as falling in this camp. She is, at the end of the day, a contractualist, which is the view that moral norms are the result of real or idealized bargaining among moral agents. Yet, the virtues play an important role in delimiting the scope and nature of moral norms in Foot's contractualist view. This chapter lays out Foot's virtue theory and outlines its role in moral philosophy.

Chapter 5 discusses Foot's contributions in the area of normative and applied ethics. The main preoccupation of Foot's interventions in these areas is determining the proper way of thinking about the demands of justice and benevolence. Justice, she thinks, may forbid us to do something that could save a greater number of people if the action would require us to deliberately kill a smaller number. This stand is part of her overall nonconsequentialism, which is the view that the rightness or wrongness of our actions is not determined solely by the goodness or badness of their consequences.

Chapter 6 discusses Foot's late ethical naturalism, as elaborated in her *Natural Goodness* and several essays. Her approach in this period focuses on an understanding of living things that appears, at least to some, to be at odds with the prevailing views in biology. These objections to her work are mistaken, as I illustrate in my own interpretation and defense of Foot's naturalism.

In Chapter 7, I look at Foot's treatment of the issue of immoralism, which is the denial that we have reason to be moral. I examine her writings on the work of Friedrich Nietzsche over the span of her career, and argue that, for the most part, Nietzsche's views are much closer to Foot's than she is, perhaps, willing to acknowledge. These two moral philosophers are actually allies in a program of post Christian moral reform.

Finally, in Chapter 8, I make some critical observations about Foot's Wittgensteinian metaphilosophical commitments. These prevented her from regarding her moral philosophy as a platform for social reform. I also point out some connections between her moral philosophy and that of other significant recent moral philosophers such as John Rawls and T. M. Scanlon.

CHAPTER ONE

Naturalism and analytic moral philosophy from Moore to Hare

*"Looking back . . . one may be surprised and a little sad,
that this particular conflict, about 'fact and value', has
occupied so much of our time. We seem to have rushed
on to the field without waiting to map the territory
supposedly in dispute, ready to die for some thesis
about commendation or approval, about pro-attitudes or
evaluation before anyone had done much detailed work on
the specific, and very different, concepts involved." (TE 12)*

In this chapter, I will discuss the philosophical context of Philippa
Foot's early writings. In her early work, she argues that moral
judgments characterize persons or actions as good, bad, right,
or wrong in view of the impact of the person's dispositions or
actions on human well-being. In taking this approach, Foot
advocates a form of naturalism, which is the view that moral
judgments describe facts about the world that we observe through
our senses. In Foot's view, moral judgments are a distinctive class
of judgments because of their subject matter, and that subject
matter is the world described by the natural sciences. Foot's

naturalism conflicts with the view that was dominant at the time—noncogntivism. For noncognitivists, moral judgments are distinguished from other judgments, not by their subject matter, but because they stand in an essential connection to attitudes of approval or disapproval and in that they are used in distinctive ways, for example, to bring about similar attitudes in others. These views, for which I will use the standard name "noncognitivism," in turn emerged from a response to the moral philosophy of G. E. Moore. Moore argued stridently against all forms of naturalism. Yet, like Foot, he thought that moral judgments are about a distinct subject matter. For Moore, moral judgments are about what will bring about the most good, using the word "good" in a distinctive sense. As Moore is often read, "good" in this special sense designates a nonnatural property belonging to a Platonic realm that, though, separate from the natural world, still somehow pertains to whatever we call "good." As we will see, although Moore's argument against naturalism was widely accepted by philosophers in the early to mid-twentieth century, his non-naturalism was seen as abhorrent because it invoked a mysterious non-natural property standing in an equally mysterious relation to the natural world.[1] Noncognitivism is an attempt to avoid the alleged problems of naturalism without the supposed mysteries of Moore's non-naturalism.

Moore: Analysis against naturalism

Foot claims that G. E. Moore's moral philosophy set the stage for her early work (TE 1). Indeed, Moore's 1903 *Principia Ethica* is widely viewed as the starting point for all analytic moral philosophy.[2] Moore's *Principia* is consequential for all subsequent analytic moral philosophy in two ways. First, methodologically, Moore establishes the possibility of treating questions of metaethics independently of normative issues.[3] Much moral philosophy through the 50 years after *Principia* appeared focuses on metaethics—specifically on the question of the relation of facts and value. This agenda is not only the result of Moore's methodological innovation of separating metaethical issues from normative ethics, but also reflects the influence of his arguments within metaethics. Second, Moore's moral philosophy is consequential in that he made an argument against naturalism in ethics that many moral philosophers regard as conclusive. As we will see in what follows, Foot's moral philosophy is influenced by both of these aspects of Moore's views.

Moral philosophy before Moore had certainly offered views on metaethical issues; yet, Moore's approach to moral philosophy is pioneering in that it treats questions concerning the meaning of "good" separately from questions about which things are good. By separating the questions "What does 'good' mean?" and "Which things are good?" Moore launched analytic moral philosophy and, for better or worse, split the enterprise of moral philosophy into two sub-disciplines. As we will see, the separation of metaethics and normative ethics leads some to believe that metaethics could be pursued with neutrality toward the various values one might hold, and because of this apparent neutrality, some philosophers take metaethics to be a more scientific enterprise than normative ethics. For Moore, unlike those influenced by him, the task of figuring out the meaning of "good" was "of the last [i.e., highest] importance" because failure to sort out such matters had been the "*cause* of the acceptance of false principles . . ."[4] For him, then, metaethics is no neutral theoretical science, but is itself an endeavor with practical consequences.

In Moore's view, moral philosophers before him had overlooked a crucial question. While treating the question "Which types of conduct are good?" they had overlooked the question of the meaning of the word "good" in general. Hence, they tended to generalize, from the meaning of the word in the context of "good conduct" to all contexts, with disastrous results. Without asking what "good" means generally, they identified "good" with one of the salient properties of good conduct, for example, producing pleasure. Moore thinks that this is analogous to the mistake one makes when identifying the meaning of "yellow" with reflecting light waves of a certain wavelength.[5] For though it may well be that all yellow things reflect light of certain wavelengths, that is not what "yellow" means. Likewise, though all good actions may produce pleasure, "producing pleasure" is not the meaning of "good." Moore therefore proposes to ask—what is the meaning of the word "good" itself?

His answer to this question is—"good" cannot be defined. By this, Moore means to say that that "good" cannot be shown to be synonymous with concepts that identify other properties, either natural or supernatural. "Good," like "yellow," is a simple notion.[6] This claim certainly suggests that Moore identifies "good" as a distinctive non-natural property, but one must determine first how one establishes the sweeping negative conclusion that no definition of "good" is adequate. To establish this conclusion, he uses what is now called the "open question argument." This argument points out the difference between asking "That may be pleasant, but is it pleasant?' which is nonsense, and "That may be pleasant, but it is good?' which is clearly meaningful. One who defines "good" as "pleasant" commits himself to viewing these concepts as substitutable. Yet, the open question argument shows that they are not substitutable. The two questions just quoted differ in meaning. With the open question argument, then, Moore believes he has found a way to reject any proposed definition of the good, whether it invokes natural or supernatural properties. For one who identifies goodness with preserving the survival of the species, Moore can point out that it makes sense to ask of any species-preserving action, "That may preserve the species, but is it good?' Likewise, for one who identifies goodness with conforming to the will of God, Moore says that it makes sense to ask of any case, "That may be an act in conformity with the will of God, but is it good?" The answer to one of these questions may always be "yes, it is good," so that being species-preserving or conforming to God's will is a reliable method of tracking what is good, but Moore's point stands, he thinks, by the mere fact that these questions are meaningful. They show that "good" means something different from the names of these qualities.

Anyone who defines "good" commits what Moore misleadingly calls the "naturalistic fallacy." This name is misleading in two ways—first, even those who define "good" in supernatural terms commit the naturalistic fallacy, so it is not truly a *naturalistic* fallacy. Second, it is not, strictly speaking, a fallacy, as William Frankena showed in a justly famous paper. The perception of the openness of a question on any given run at the open question argument depends on a prior conviction that there are two distinct properties rather than one. In other words, anyone who is fully convinced that "good" means "producing pleasure" will find the question "That may be pleasant, but is it good?" to be nonsensical. Hence, the argument begs the question. There is only an error—a fallacy if you like—if two distinct properties are conflated, but that is precisely what is at issue. Yet, many readers of Moore share his conviction that the questions are indeed open. Further, as Stephen Darwall has pointed out, the apparent openness of the question may stem not so much from the necessary falsehood of any attempt at defining the good, but from the fact that goodness has a connection with action, which the proposed definitions do not have. Because we are self-reflective agents, Darwall argues, we can stand back and examine any proposed value; we can ask, ought we to value that?[7] And this ability gives the open question argument its force. Although Frankena is correct that the naturalistic fallacy is not a fallacy, this is compatible with Darwall's point that the open question argument has some force against naturalism. Still, it should be noted that in the 36 years between the publication of *Principia Ethica* and Frankena's article, Moore's argument against naturalism was widely perceived as knock-down.

As mentioned above, Moore appears to commit himself to the view that "good," in the sense that is at issue in moral judgments, refers to a non-natural property. This property is not perceivable by the senses or by its causal effects on the natural world; instead, it would be detected by intellectual intuition. Indeed, this is the interpretation of Moore that Foot adopts (TE 2). To many philosophers following Moore, this view involves two objectionable claims. First, the idea that there are some properties that are not part of the natural world is at odds with the prevailing empiricist epistemology. After all, to say that there is a property apart from the natural world is to say that there is something that does not have any causal interactions with the natural world, and so could not be understood in terms of empirically funded scientific laws. Second, the appeal to intuition seems to ignore the fact that people have different intuitions about what is good. Admitting those disagreements, it is not clear that there could be a method for resolving moral disputes rationally. Parties to a disagreement would seem to be left with thumping their chests and appealing to their separate intuitions.

Although this damning assessment of Moore is widely shared, it is not clear that it is based on a charitable interpretation of Moore's claims. As Robert Shaver argues, it is possible to read Moore as denying that goodness is a natural concept, but not denying that it is a natural property.[8] That is, the concept of goodness describes a feature of the natural world that is not accessible to the natural sciences. Goodness cannot be *analyzed* in terms of any one natural property, according to Moore, but that does not mean that goodness is not natural. This interpretation of Moore's view turns on distinguishing an analytic connection between goodness and a natural property, on the one hand, and a constitutive connection between goodness and natural properties, on the other hand. In this view, any natural property constitutive of goodness in a given case may not always be sufficient to make something good, and such a property may not be the only property that makes something good. Hence, in Shaver's interpretation, non-naturalism rejects the idea that moral matters can be settled scientifically, but does not posit a property or class of properties that is metaphysically irreconcilable with a commitment to scientific naturalism.

As for the epistemological problems with Moore's view, Shaver argues that although Moore leaves himself open to these charges, these problems are not inherent to Moore's position. The non-naturalist can appeal to precisely the same justifications that naturalists appeal to—most importantly, systematizing common sense moral judgments.[9] That is, the non-naturalist's appeals to intuition are not necessarily infallible, and for any intuitively plausible instance of something that is deemed good, we can ask whether that claim can be squared with other intuitions about what is good. Overall, then, Moore's non-naturalism is probably more defensible than has been generally acknowledged by those who rejected it, including Foot.

Ayer and Stevenson: Emotivism

In the widely received version of Moore's views, goodness is a property of things, albeit a property of a special kind. It is like "yellow" in being simple and indefinable. Yet, unlike yellow, it is not accessible through our senses. For those who find Moore's open question argument compelling, but who cannot accept the implications of his non-naturalism, the only solution appears to be this alternative response—to deny that goodness names any sort of property at all. They propose that we should seek to explain moral judgments by identifying a characteristic function they perform, rather than a specific class of property that they designate. Much moral philosophy understands moral judgments to have a descriptive function. In such a view, some moral judgments describe a thing as featuring the property of goodness. Yet, clearly not all meaningful language *describes* the world; for example, we use language to express feelings (e.g., "How wonderful!") and to command (e.g.,

"Open the door!"). These other functions of language do not ascribe properties. In the former case, the words express a positive feeling or attitude toward something. Similarly, the latter does not ascribe a property, but rather, commands someone to do something. By exploiting these disparate functions of language, some moral philosophers hope to avoid problems with descriptive theories of moral judgment, such as the difficulties with Moore's view under its standard interpretation.

For these moral philosophers, working around 30 years after Moore's *Principia*, moral language serves a purpose that combines an expressive and a commanding function. A. J. Ayer's 1936 *Language, Truth and Logic* contained an early, though brief exposition of this view of moral judgments. He writes:

> . . . if I say to someone, 'You acted wrongly in stealing that money,' I am not stating anything more than if I had simply said, 'You stole that money.' In adding that this action is wrong I am not making any further statement about it. I am simply evincing my moral disapproval of it.[10]

We see in this passage that there is, in Ayer's view, a descriptive component to a moral judgment (in this case—"you stole the money"). However, such a descriptive statement is clearly not a moral judgment. What distinguishes a moral judgment from an ordinary descriptive statement is the expression of an attitude toward the descriptive content. Further, at least some moral judgments convey commands. According to Ayer, the sentence, "It is your duty to tell the truth" is equivalent to "Tell the truth!"[11] The view expounded in Ayer's treatise came to be known as emotivism because it defined moral judgments in terms of a function of expressing feelings or attitudes. Note that the moral language does not *describe* feelings that the speaker has; it expresses them. Contrast—"I approve of x" with "hooray for x!" The former describes my attitude; the latter expresses it.

C. L. Stevenson, in his 1944 *Ethics and Language* and a number of papers that appeared between 1937 and 1962, developed the idea in Ayer's brief discussion of emotivism into a complete metaethical theory. For Stevenson, moral terms are used in two central ways. In the first use, terms like "good" are used to say "I approve of x. Do so as well." Stevenson is careful to point out that this translation of "good" is at best crude, and for reasons to be discussed, he came to think of all such translations as seriously misleading.[12] Nevertheless, the translation captures, according to Stevenson, something of what he calls the emotive meaning of moral terms, which he defines as, "the power that the word acquires, on account of its history in emotional situations, to evoke or directly express attitudes, as distinct from describing or designating them."[13] So, in Stevenson's view, "good" is, in part, supposed to express my positive attitude toward something. Unfortunately, "I approve of x" does not quite capture that. Instead, it expresses my belief that I have a positive attitude toward something, and thus the two claims must have quite a different meaning, as Stevenson later came to realize. After all, "I approve of x" is a descriptive claim about my psychology, and there is a specific type of evidence that would support or undermine that claim. This is quite unlike an utterance that actually expresses my approval of x, such as "Hooray for x!" Since that exclamation is purely expressive, we cannot gather evidence for or against it. For utterances that express attitudes, the whole idea of evidence seems out of place. Likewise, the second part of the translation, "do so as well," suggests that saying "x is good" has an imperatival function, but Stevenson was wary of this claim even as he stated it. After all, an actual command to adopt an attitude is likely to backfire. Something subtler is going on with "good," as Stevenson readily admitted. To say that something is good, then, suggests to another that she adopt the speaker's positive attitude as well, and it is to exert a causal, rather than rational effect on its hearer. In exuding my positive attitude toward something linguistically, I hope to bring you to the same positive attitude by means of verbal suggestion.

The second application of moral terms Stevenson analyzes is when speaker defines her moral terms; for example, when utilitarians define goodness as "maximizing happiness," they are engaged in a distinctive use of language that Stevenson calls "persuasive definition." In a persuasive definition, the speaker attempts to fix the emotive meaning of moral terms to specific ranges of descriptive content.[14] In Stevenson's view, though all normative ethics is persuasive definition, we are often not aware that this is what we are doing. In Stevenson's view, the meaning of "good" is not tied to any specific descriptive content. From the standpoint of metaethics, all definitions that have been offered of "good" are equally valid. Yet, there is a temptation to think of persuasive definitions as having a logical or scientific foundation that they cannot have, according to Stevenson.[15]

In fact, no moral judgment can have a rational basis, according to Stevenson. Or, to put the point somewhat more carefully, rational methods apply in ethics only inasmuch as beliefs are concerned. Say, I am a utilitarian and I approve of whatever I see as maximizing overall happiness. The question that will constantly confront me as a utilitarian is a factual one—what is the best way to maximize happiness? Clearly, this question calls for weighing evidence by scientific means. But if a utilitarian attempts to persuade a non-utilitarian to adopt this principle, rational debate may well break down, and in that case, we will be left with persuasion aimed at bringing about a change of attitude. For Stevenson, that is a task in which I must simply apply whatever rhetorical means seem appropriate to me. Most often, he thinks, I will appeal to something toward which I know you to have a positive attitude, and then try to associate what I value with that thing; it may be that there is a causal relation between them, and then we are back to beliefs where rational methods apply. Otherwise, I may have to resort to nonrational methods such as using colorful language or stamping my feet, with the hope that I will bring about a change in your attitudes. As Stevenson puts it, "*Any* statement about *any* matter of fact which *any* speaker considers likely to alter attitudes may be adduced as a reason for or against an ethical judgment."[16] Here, the meaning of "reason" is revised to an extent that strains its ordinary meaning; it is not supporting evidence for a claim, but rather the cause of adopting an attitude. On reflection, Stevenson's claim might seem rather alarming. After all, Hitler was remarkably successful in winning over many people to his atrocious cause with his rhetoric; he also effectively used propaganda to persuade people to follow his cause. In Stevenson's view, however, all moralists can be called propagandists, provided that we suspend the usual emotive force of that term. Moralists and propagandists are both engaged in an attempt to change other people's attitudes. Hitler was forwarding a program that we deplore, so we call him a propagandist, with a negative emotive charge whereas Martin Luther King, Jr., say, was engaged in activism on behalf of causes that we approve of, so we call him a moralist, with a positive charge.

Still, emotivism is troubling in that, if it is true, we have no rationally justifiable grounds for our moral condemnation of

Hitler. Why, then, were Ayer and Stevenson drawn to emotivism? It has three main attractions. First, it avoids the metaphysical and epistemological problems associated with Moore's non-naturalism. After all, goodness in this view does not refer to any property, and therefore, this approach would nicely avoid metaphysical and epistemological issues that plague moral philosophy when it takes a descriptive stance on the distinctive content of moral judgments. Second, it does not fall to the open question argument. To see this point, it is essential to remember that emotivists are not defining "good" as "whatever I approve of." In stating "x is good," I am not stating the factual judgment "I approve of x," but instead, I am *emoting*, expressing an attitude to x; therefore saying "x is good" is equivalent to saying "Hooray for x!" Since this view does not define goodness in terms of natural or supernatural properties, it agrees with Moore's view that it is always an open question whether possession of some natural or supernatural property makes something good. Finally, emotivism captures something intuitively true about the relation of goodness to choice. In Moore's view, calling something good is identifying a property it has, and therefore it is a matter of making an assertion. In such a view, describing something as good can be done with the indifferent, contemplative attitude with which one can describe the craters on the surface of the Moon. This seems to miss the point of calling something good, which is to praise it and to advocate choosing it. The emotivist view captures the apparent practical role of calling something good; as Stevenson memorably puts it, the difference between traditional views and the emotivist view is like the difference between "describing a desert and irrigating it."[17] In Stevenson's view, ethical terms are "*instruments* in the complicated interplay and readjustment of human interests."[18]

The emotivist view advocated by Ayer and Stevenson represents a sea change in moral philosophy, which was inspired by still broader changes in philosophy, especially the philosophy of language. Moral philosophy before emotivism takes language to be primarily descriptive and understands meaning in terms of truth conditions. As Ludwig Wittgenstein put it in his *Tractatus Logico-Philosophicus* (1922), "To understand a proposition means to know what is the case, if it is true."[19] Such a view captures something central about the meaning of assertions; if we understand an assertion, we know when it is true. Yet, in defining meaning in terms of truth conditions, Wittgenstein effectively takes asserting to be the primary function of language. The

Tractatus, however, gave expression to a widely shared conception of what is essential to the meaning of language. After writing the *Tractatus*, Wittgenstein began to question the adequacy of his earlier views. He began to think that language has uses far beyond asserting what is the case, and though these uses had, no doubt, occurred to him earlier, he began to believe that he had not taken them seriously enough; he began to see them as pertinent to how one should formulate a philosophical account of meaning. He shared these ideas, which he formulated in the late 1920s, with an influential group of empiricist philosophers and scientists known as the Vienna Circle, and through them, his ideas gained a broader audience. Wittgenstein's insistence on taking the nondescriptive functions of language seriously was heard by moral philosophers such as Ayer and Stevenson. Moreover, Wittgenstein's work on these matters was pivotal in that it demonstrated a way to account for these nondescriptive uses of language through examining how the varieties of language define various kinds of activity, which he called "language games."[20]

Stevenson was undertaking just such a pragmatic analysis. Stevenson saw moral judgments as a language game in which we seek to exert an influence on each other's attitudes. His 1944 *Ethics and Language* features imagined but realistic conversations thought by Stevenson to capture various styles of ethical language. For example:

A: The proposed tax bill is on the whole very bad.

B: I know little about it, but have been inclined to favor it on the ground that higher taxes are preferable to further borrowing.

A: It provides for a sales-tax on a number of necessities and reduces income-tax exemptions to an incredibly low figure.

B: I had not realized that. I must study the bill, and perhaps I shall agree with you in opposing it.[21]

For Stevenson, this passage is typical of moral language in that A is attempting to persuade B to adopt his negative attitude toward the tax bill by pointing to features of the bill he believes to be disagreeable to his interlocutor. In one way, it is refreshing to see recognizable conversations brought into moral philosophy; yet, the example misleadingly obscures the extent to which Stevenson is advocating a dramatic revision to what we regard as moral language. That is because, in his view, moral discourse encompasses any language deemed by a speaker likely to change someone else's attitudes, and that is certainly an unusual and alarmingly broad conception of moral language.

In an important discussion of Stevenson's views, Stanley Cavell points out two ways in which Stevenson's theory of morality and moral discourse is counterintuitive. First, we typically think that there is a difference between convincing someone to do something with reasons and bringing him to do it by effecting a change of mind using any means whatsoever. Stevenson's view obviously collapses this distinction.[22] In his view, moral language is a matter of *causing* someone to adopt a different attitude, which is a case of nonrational suggestion. Reasons operate remarkably differently in moral language than in language that describes the world. Stevenson takes emotive meaning, rather than descriptive content, to be essential to moral judgments. In descriptive language, reasons support the truth of a statement, and so, reasons in this sense do not have a role in moral language, in Stevenson's view. One cannot be convinced of the truth of "It is good to donate to charities," as one can be convinced of the truth that the Human Immunodeficiency Virus causes AIDS. Rather, one can only be manipulated into adopting a positive attitude toward donating to charities by means of such a moral judgment. Further, according to Stevenson, any statement that is likely to bring about a change of attitude counts as a reason.[23] And this view is surely revisionary, though Stevenson did not take it to be so. As Cavell puts across this point:

> . . . what such a theory says, in effect, is that there is no theoretical difference between persuading someone to do something by convincing him that he ought to, *using reasons which convince you*, and persuading him by appeals to his fears, your prestige, or another's money. It may *in fact* be the case that the latter grounds are always decisive, that no such difference is manifest in the practice of a given society; Thrasymachus and Marx, among others, thought that. But then they *knew* they were attacking morality and society as a whole.[24]

It might seem extreme to characterize Stevenson's view as "attacking morality and society as a whole." Yet, consider that Stevenson's view will call any language "moral language" that the speaker believes likely to change another's attitude. In such a view, lies, abuse, and blackmail may count as moral language, and that is surely a revisionary conception of moral language, even if not, on that account, wrong. A second point Cavell makes about Stevenson's account is that it breaks the connection between morality and justice. For, in Stevenson's view, morality involves one's own attitudes and does not require taking into account the attitudes of others, except when it is relevant to effectively bringing about someone's agreement. That is also disturbing. Stevenson attempts to provide a detached theoretical account of the nature of morality by way of characterizing the meaning of moral judgments; following Moore, he has attempted to pursue that characterization independently of weighing in on which things are good. Yet, as Cavell rightly discerns, Stevenson is not able to do that. His views on the nature of moral judgment actually reflect values that Stevenson, no doubt, does not wish to advocate. Metaethics is, in fact, as Moore himself thought, of the highest importance.

Shifting away from characterizing moral judgment as essentially descriptive also changes our desiderata for a moral theory. With a view such as Moore's, in which we are characterizing goodness as a property, the concern is to determine whether we can offer a plausible metaphysical account of such a property, fitting it within the world described by the natural sciences. Also, from such an account, we want a plausible way in which we can identify which things are good and resolve disputes about which things are good. We must have different expectations of the noncognitivist views, however, since they claim that goodness does not name a property. For noncognitivist views, we want to know whether the account of moral discourse fits with what we understand morality to be, or, if it suggests revision, suggests an acceptable revision. Here, Stevenson's account appears to falter before Cavell's objections. Yet, Stevenson's approach was innovative and far from the last attempt to provide an account of moral language without appealing to moral properties, and as we will see throughout this study, many of Foot's best insights came from reflecting on these attempts.

R. M. Hare: Prescriptivism

R. M. Hare was one of the most important targets of criticism in Foot's early work. His output, almost entirely on moral philosophy, was considerable, and his views developed and changed between his first book, *The Language of Morals* (1952) and his last book, *Objective Prescriptions* (1999). In order to prepare for a discussion of Foot's early criticisms of noncognitivism, I will here primarily discuss Hare's early works, *The Language of Morals* and *Freedom and Reason* (1963), with occasional references to points in which he later qualified, amended, or simply stated his views more clearly.

Hare built on the emotivism of Ayer and Stevenson. Indeed, according to Hare, Stevenson's distinction between descriptive and emotive meaning was "perhaps the single most important contribution in this century to the understanding of moral language."[25] Yet, Hare also thought that Stevenson took some serious missteps. Most notably, he thought Stevenson was wrong in taking moral language to have a causal function. As Hare states in *The Language of Morals*, "The processes of *telling* someone to do something, and *getting* him to do it, are quite distinct, logically, from each other."[26] In Hare's view, moral language is prescriptive, but not suggestive in the way Stevenson proposes. That is, a moral judgment tells us to do something, but it is not its function to make us do that thing. In this way, Hare hopes to distance himself from some of the troubling aspects of Stevenson's views, namely, Stevenson's inability to distinguish moral judgment from propaganda. Hare retains from Stevenson the idea that moral judgments do not describe; he coins the term "descriptivism" to name the views that take the function of moral judgment to be descriptive. His view is that the role of moral judgment is prescriptive, and so, he terms his own view "prescriptivism." To be prescriptive means to command or to entail a command. Yet, no imperative can be entailed by any set of statements that does not contain an imperative.[27] Hence, Hare believes, in order to capture the prescriptive function of moral judgments, we must take moral judgments to be imperatives. Further, imperatives are governed by logical rules, just as statements are, and Hare takes part of his task to be setting out the logical rules that govern imperatives. In so doing, he hopes to show that moral judgments are responsive to reasons in a manner that parallels factual statements, while acknowledging the distinct prescriptive function of moral judgments. As he puts it, his aim is "to find a rationalist kind of nondescriptivism."[28]

Like Ayer and Stevenson, Hare argues for a divide between descriptive meaning and evaluative or prescriptive meaning. Let us examine how he does this in the case of "good," at least in his early work. Hare believes that "good" has a function of commending, and he holds that if the meaning of "good" were identical with some descriptive content, it would inevitably lose its commendatory function.[29] Saying that something has a certain property certainly seems distinct from commending it for having that property. Suppose we think being good is identical with having a disposition to cause pleasure. To say that something is good then means that I am saying that it tends to produce pleasure. Yet, describing something as pleasant is distinct from commending it for being pleasant, and if so, something would be lost through the identification of "good" with pleasure. Indeed, identifying "good" with any property will bring about a similar loss.

Further, consider saying that a knife is a good knife and saying that a car is a good car. In each case, there are ranges of criteria that apply for when a knife is a good knife and when a car a good car. Yet, the criteria for each are quite different. Still, we do not need, Hare claims, to learn the meaning of the word "good" anew with each new category to which we might apply it. Indeed, we can understand what it means to call something good without understanding the criteria for calling a thing of that sort "good."[30] Whatever we call good, Hare thinks, we commend, and to commend is to recommend choosing that thing. Commendation is not just the function of the word "good"; it is the meaning of the word "good." The meaning is distinct from the criteria for goodness, which vary depending on what class of thing we are considering. It would not even do to propose a lengthy definition of goodness that conjoins all the different criteria for all the different classes of good things that there are. That is because, as Hare points out, there is something constant underlying the application of goodness to all of these classes that we would miss. Furthermore, if we do not hold that the meaning of the word "good" is distinct from the criteria of its application, we foreclose the possibility of revision to our standards of goodness.[31] This is a significant element of Hare's criticism of descriptivists—they fix the meaning of "good" to specific criteria and thereby undermine the possibility of revision.[32] They fix the meaning of "good" to the criteria of goodness accepted by a society, and this raises three additional worries. First, it seems that we have, in fact, changed our views about what is good, and one wonders how this is possible under the descriptivist view, unless it is simply an inexplicable, arbitrary shift in usage. Second, different cultures use the term "good" in different ways, and therefore descriptivists invite the charge of cultural relativism, which is worrisome because it undercuts the possibility of discussing how we ought to behave with wide ranges of people, that is, with whomever might have different criteria of goodness, and so mean something different by "good."[33] Finally, it is not clear how a descriptivist is going to capture the action-guiding aspect of value terms. Whatever criteria we have for "good," in whatever culture we belong to, it is still the case that "good" on all these different definitions is supposed to guide choice, and it is not obvious how the descriptivist can account for this.

According to Hare, then, there is a constant possibility of revising our accepted standards of goodness by a process that Hare explicitly likens to Stevenson's notion of persuasive definition. In proposing the criteria for goodness, I am proposing that you too commend what falls under my proposed criteria, and that you see those things as choice worthy. In saying "all lightweight knives with durable sharp blades are good," I am proposing that you accept this as a criterion, and, if accepted, this criterion entails an imperative of the form "let me choose such knives," and when the time comes, I will fill that out with "here is such a knife; let me choose it." In this way, evaluative judgments are action guiding, according to Hare.

Yet, one wonders whether Hare's view holds any advantages over Stevenson's view if both views allow the moral reformer to lay down any criteria whatsoever for goodness. How is he offering us a distinctively *rational* form of nondescriptivism? Hare thinks that in making an evaluative judgment, we are implicitly making a universal judgment.[34] To deem something is good is not only to say that this particular thing is good, but that anything similar to it is good as well. To say one thing is good while another similar to it is not, one must point out some relevant difference between them. Hence, according to Hare, our evaluative judgments must be universalizable; when we make a moral judgment, we are saying that this is how to act in circumstances like this, and we must be committed to accepting the same claim in all relevantly similar circumstances. This idea is sometimes also called "supervenience" inasmuch as it amounts to the claim that goodness supervenes on some set of natural properties. Hare is certainly not the first to point this out; yet, Hare integrated it within a nondescriptivist framework and argued that it had the power to capture the way that moral judgments are responsive to reasons. In this, he likened his view to that of Immanuel Kant. As Hare puts it:

> To ask whether I ought to do A in these circumstances is (to borrow Kantian language with a small though important modification) to ask whether or not I will that doing A in such circumstances should become a universal law . . . the same question could be put in other words by asking 'What attitude shall I adopt and recommend toward doing A in such circumstances?' for 'attitude', if it means anything, means a principle of action.[35]

So far, this seems to commit us only to consistency in our evaluative judgments, and even Stevenson embraced this requirement. As becomes clear in *Freedom and Reason*, Hare believes that universalizability requires us to take up the perspective of others, and to affirm our commitment to a principle in view of the fact that individuals have different desires. Drawing from the Gospel of Matthew, Hare asks us to imagine someone (B) who owes a debt to someone (C), and who has someone in his debt (A). Can this person endorse that the person who owes him money should be imprisoned? He can rationally endorse this view only if he is willing to be imprisoned for his own debt. For, Hare claims, to say "I ought to put A into prison for the debt he owes me" contains a commitment to a principle "Anyone who is in my position ought to put his debtor into prison if he does not pay." Yet, B is in the same situation with C, so if he affirms this principle, he too should be thrown into prison. He must either reject the principle or affirm that he too ought to be thrown into prison. Of course, it is logically possible for B to say that he ought to be thrown into prison, but Hare assumes that most people so situated will reject such a principle, if they think through the implications of their judgment as a universal principle.[36] What about a case in which a judge is about to sentence a criminal? In that case, should the judge reject a prison sentence, since he too could be the criminal? Here, Hare says "no" because there are more than two parties involved; the judge is charged with the enforcement of a community's laws, and he must universalize to all the parties involved.[37] Because of the preferences of the broader community for justice and protection from criminals, taking the perspective of others will compel the judge to imprison a dangerous criminal. Hare believes that the requirement to universalize our judgments enforces a utilitarian standard. For, in taking up the position of other people affected by our actions, we must give equal weight to their preferences, and, Hare thinks, we must take into account the strength of those preferences as well. The result is that moral reasoning encourages us to maximize the satisfaction of everyone's preferences, and this is a sort of utilitarianism known as "preference utilitarianism."

It is important to emphasize two points here. First, Hare is not affirming utilitarianism as a substantive moral doctrine. Rather, he believes that utilitarian reasoning simply is a part of the logic of moral judgments. It is because all moral judgments are prescriptive and implicitly universal that we are required to adopt the perspectives of others and give weight to their preferences. Second, Hare acknowledges that it is logically possible to consider the preferences of others and, at the same time, simply to reject those preferences. This is to endorse a kind of nonutilitarian ideal. He gives the loaded name of "fanatic" to individuals disposed to this sort of reasoning. Hare's primary examples of individuals who reject utilitarian reasoning are the Nazis; they endorse morally reprehensible ideals that they are willing to advocate even in the face of the hypothetical possibility of being the victim of their own cruelty. Hare thinks that many people who endorse such views have simply failed to vividly imagine the situation of those who are or would be affected by their racist principles, and that the best way of changing their minds is to attempt to engage their imaginations in the contemplation of being such an individual, as inspiring novelists and rhetoricians can sometimes do.[38] Of course, to call those who reject utilitarian principles "fanatics" is to engage in name calling rather than argumentation. It may well be morally commendable to adopt principles that one would not give up even for the sake of maximizing the satisfaction of preferences. For example, some nonconsequentialists (including Foot) argue that it is unjust to kill one person to save five; in that view, it would not be permissible for me to drive over one person in order to get to five people who are in danger from drowning, for example. Hare's approach would classify those with such reasonable moral principles, and not only the Nazis, as "fanatics."

Yet, like Stevenson, Hare believes, at least in his writings before his 1981 book, *Moral Thinking*, that his theory is morally neutral. It does not endorse any single moral view. He holds that even if it does not reach specific moral conclusions, his theory is still significant because it demonstrates the possibility of moral disagreement and rational debate about morality. He believes that his theory should give us hope that fanaticism will disappear and be replaced by a morally superior liberalism; that is because, to the extent that we are brought in contact with the consequences of our actions and vivid imagination of the perspectives of others, we will stop insisting on adhering to our ideals in the face of the fact that they thwart the strong preferences of others. Whereas Stevenson equates advocacy of moral causes with propaganda, Hare thinks that one of the primary functions of moral philosophy is to defend us from propaganda.[39] It does this by illuminating the logic of moral judgment. In particular, Hare has in mind the fact that it alerts us to persuasive definitions of moral terms. That is, it makes us aware that they *are* persuasive definitions, and that the prescriptions the definitions lead us to endorse are not etched in nature. For Hare, naturalists are not merely wrong, but morally dangerous because naturalism denies our freedom to reflectively endorse principles by making it seem as though some evaluative views are simply the case.

Does Hare succeed in offering a noncognitivist view that squares better than Stevenson's emotivism with what we take morality to be? Surely, he evades some of Stevenson's most obvious problems that stem from taking moral language to have a causal function. Yet, many philosophers, including Foot, insist that he did not succeed in capturing central features of moral judgment. As Foot points out, Hare must accept that there could be moral eccentrics who argue that a man was good because "he clasped and unclasped his hands and never turned N.N.E. after turning S.S.W." (VV 111; see also WPMP 104). Foot holds that Hare has articulated a "private enterprise theory of moral criteria" that is entirely artificial, inasmuch as it divorces the meaning of moral terms from the context that gives them a moral sense. Foot argues that the relevant context would connect the terms to human good or harm (VV 106, 120). Hare admits that he is committed to viewing the eccentrics as moral eccentrics. He believes he is right to do so because, as he puts it, "a crazy moral judgment is still a moral judgment" (OP 90).[40] Yet, this misses Foot's point. For, in her view, one certainly can make outlandish moral judgments, provided that the context for a connection with human good and harm is present. For instance, it is difficult to see how "one ought not to wear brightly colored clothes" could be a moral judgment. Yet, Foot points out that it certainly can be, if one fills in the requisite background, for instance, the view that wearing brightly colored cloths is ostentatious (WPMP 105). The concept of ostentation indicates a kind of vice; to be ostentatious is detrimental to good social relationships, which are part of the human good. Hence, it is possible to fill out a context within what initially seems trivial—wearing bright clothes—so it makes sense as something someone might morally condemn. Note that according to Hare, it is not necessary to draw this connection to the human good, and that is why Foot regards Hare's view as engaging in a private enterprise view of moral judgment. Her point is that absent a connection with the human good, the sincere affirmation of a universally prescriptive statement does not suffice to make a judgment into a moral judgment. She is opposing the view that an individual can privately make a universal prescription into a moral judgment simply through adopting a certain sort of attitude.

This exchange between Hare and Foot will be further explored in the next chapter, but before continuing to explore that debate, there is a related, important criticism of Hare that deserves mention. This criticism was set out by Iris Murdoch in a paper entitled "Vision and Choice in Morality" (1956).[41] Murdoch's basic point is like Cavell's criticism of Stevenson—Hare does not achieve the neutrality he claims for his view. According to Murdoch, Hare fails to recognize that the logic of moral judgments he presents actually belongs to his own substantive moral commitments. Because Hare's portrayal of the logic of moral judgments belongs to a particular moral view, Murdoch believes that Hare's view cannot be taken as the only "structural model of morality."[42] As Murdoch puts it:

> There are people whose fundamental moral belief is that we all lie in the same empirical and rationally comprehensible world and that morality is the adoption of universal and openly defensible rules of conduct. There are other people whose fundamental belief is that we live in a world whose mystery transcends us and that morality is the exploration of that mystery in so far as it concerns each individual. It is only by sharpening the universality model to a point of extreme abstraction that it can be made to cover both views.[43]

Notice that Murdoch does say that Hare's view *can* be made to cover both cases. Hare takes pains to emphasize the neutrality of his view by showing that he can accommodate the reasoning of a Nazi. Yet, there is reason to think that in reconstructing a Nazi's reasoning to conform to his model of moral reasoning, Hare has distorted the reasoning out of recognition by actual Nazis. As Cora Diamond puts across this point:

> Hare presents us with a Nazi who has been reconstructed in significant ways, to make his moral views universalizable. His Nazi is not so much an anti-Semite as an anti-everybody-who-has-certain-characteristics. . . . The requirement of passionate devotion to Germany and its 'revolution' was not the application to Germany of a universal principle requiring passionate devotion to one's country.[44]

So, although Hare can reconstruct Nazi reasoning to conform to his structural model, there is a fundamental moral difference between his reconstructed Nazi and an actual Nazi. The actual Nazi, especially an ideologically sophisticated one, deliberately rejects the style of universalized reasoning that Hare believes to be morally neutral. Perhaps Hare could respond by saying that the Nazi, inasmuch as he does reject such reasoning, shows himself to be deficiently rational, but then he must become suspicious of the neutrality of the term "rational." For, if this were Hare's response, it would appear that he is saying that we *should* reason in this way and in that case, he is giving us what he would regard as a moral recommendation, and his conception of rationality would not be morally neutral.

Murdoch believes that, despite Hare's claim to neutrality, a specific moral view shapes his understanding of moral concepts and that this understanding, in turn, lies behind Hare's view that naturalism or descriptivism makes a philosophical error. In Hare's understanding of moral concepts, they designate a specific range of publicly accessible facts (their descriptive content) plus a recommendation (their emotive or prescriptive meaning). "Good," according to Hare, is entirely flexible in its descriptive meaning, but fixed in its prescriptive meaning. For Hare, one is free to call anything whatsoever "good," provided that, in doing so, one affirms a principle by which things with such-and-such properties are recommended.

By contrast, "courage," for Hare, is fixed in both its descriptive and evaluative meaning—it commends a certain range of behavior. One who wishes to reject the value of courageous acts must reject the term "courage." We do that by translating the term "courage" into neutral descriptive language and then adopting a different principled stance toward that behavior. According to Murdoch, Hare's view of moral concepts encapsulates a moral commitment to the freedom of the agent. For any concept that contains an evaluation, we can translate that concept into descriptive content and take a principled stance on whether we share the evaluation in the concept. There is no part of the world that is accessible only via concepts such as "courage"; there are only morally neutral facts that may be more or less difficult to access. Provided I am adequately informed, I can make a free decision of principle. By contrast, Murdoch believes that there are positive moral conceptions, such as those of a Marxist or a Christian, whose moral commitments are inseparable from the concepts they deploy—concepts such as hope and love.[45] In such views, these concepts are crucial to describing a reality of moral facts, facts about the world as the holder of these views finds it. According to Murdoch, "the true naturalist . . . is one who *believes* that as moral beings we are immersed in a reality which transcends us and that moral progress consists in awareness of this reality and submission to its purposes."[46] The idea that there is a logical error in moving from facts to values reflects, in Murdoch's view, Hare's broader commitment to viewing the world as containing nothing but facts of a certain sort. In short, she sees Hare's philosophy, including his conception of the underlying logic of morality as the expression of a Liberal Protestant moral conception, in that it values freedom, toleration, and embraces an empiricist conception of facts denuded of moral significance. If she is right, this debunks Hare's claim to have uncovered *the* underlying logic of moral judgments, for there are legitimate moral views that do not conform to his structural model of morality. As we will see in the next chapter, it is no coincidence that Foot devotes her first book to Iris Murdoch. Foot's early writings make a careful case for the point that facts can generate evaluative conclusions, an underdeveloped aspect of Murdoch's argument. Foot thereby takes on a central issue for defending the idea that naturalism is no mistake.

CHAPTER TWO

Moral concepts in Foot's early naturalism

"To many people it seems that the most notable advance in moral philosophy in the past fifty years or so has been the refutation of naturalism; and they are a little shocked that at this late date such an issue should be reopened." (VV 110)

In her first article, "The Philosopher's Defence of Morality" (1952), Foot tentatively advocated Hare's view that the criteria and meaning of "good" are wholly independent. As she states:

> . . . it would make some sense to say we had discovered a people who reversed all our moral judgments, thinking good all the things we thought bad and vice versa, but it would not make sense to report that some other race thought our blue things yellow and our yellow things blue. (PDM 313)

Yet, in an article published just two years later, Foot begins to question the sharp distinction between criteria and meaning for evaluative terms like "good" and "right." In the article, she denies that it makes sense to think of someone inverting our moral judgments, at least without a special context. If such morally inverted people can be said to possess morality at all, they would have to possess a radically different set of background beliefs connecting those inverted moral beliefs to the human good. In order to morally praise someone who wantonly kills for pleasure, one would have to believe that it is good for the person doing it, since it clearly is not good for the victim of one's aggression. For example, one might believe that uninhibited aggression is good for a person and restraints on aggression are bad for a person, and then couple this belief with an improbably nonchalant attitude toward the threat of harm to oneself and one's family from others pursuing their "good." It is difficult to imagine the possibility of a group possessing such a morality, but that may be because we find such a view of the human good so implausible. Such moral beliefs are logically possible, but it is not logically possible, Foot argues, for our beliefs to remain moral beliefs without possessing some relevance to human well-being. Further, one cannot deem anything one likes to be good for or harmful to humans; what is good for or harmful to humans is straightforwardly factual. This means that, for Foot, there is a connection between moral values and facts about what is good for or harmful to humans. In fact, Foot argues in the article that one can *deduce* evaluative conclusions from factual premises. She contends that there is no fallacy in defining the terms "right" and "wrong" in the way Jeremy Bentham did in his *Principles of Morals and Legislation* (1781), in which he claimed that the terms have no meaning apart from the principle of utility.[1] In other words, there is no logical problem with saying that an action can be right if and only if it satisfies some factual description, such as maximizing overall happiness. Although Foot rejects the naturalistic fallacy, she nevertheless disagrees with Bentham over the definition of moral terms since her own naturalism is not utilitarian, but rather, Aristotelian. She defines good conduct in terms of virtues understood as traits that tend to promote the good human life, including the good of their possessor. So, her argument for naturalism is accompanied by an argument that the virtues play a more important role in morality than previous moral philosophy had acknowledged. Although virtue terms do not have a rigidly fixed meaning, their intelligible use is restricted in domain because they must connect somehow to the human good. One cannot call someone "courageous" when he stands up to what he knows to be cardboard representations of monsters, except as a joke. The connection of our views on good and bad conduct to the virtues means that, for Foot, our evaluation of conduct turns on a conception of the human good. We praise conduct when it exhibits courage because of the connection that trait has with the human good.

In all of this work, Foot takes direct aim at the non-naturalism that dominates Anglophone moral philosophy from Moore to Hare. In this chapter, I will present her arguments for naturalism and against non-naturalism while attempting to assess them in light of some of the philosophically significant responses they have provoked since their appearance. I will argue that Foot avoids whatever force the open question argument might be assumed to possess, including Hare's revised form of the argument, and thus argue that she succeeds in defending a form of naturalism from this sort of rebuttal.

The moral hand clasper

In the previous chapter, I introduced Foot's charge against Hare—namely that he endorses a "private enterprise" theory of moral judgments. Foot's opponents believe that to make a moral judgment, it is sufficient to adopt a certain sort of attitude toward something. Hence, in such a view, to frame a moral judgment is to be in a certain sort of private mental state. To use one of Foot's classic examples, in such theories it is possible to deem it a morally good action to always clasp one's hands three times in an hour. Foot believes that this is an absurdity because one cannot make this action a good one just by adopting a certain attitude toward it. Hare believes Foot is trading on the "weaker analogues" of logical absurdity; he does not believe it is strictly logically impossible to have a moral view such as this, but rather, it is merely highly unlikely. He compares it to someone claiming to lift a one-ton weight with his bare hands; although it is highly improbable, we know what someone who makes this claim means, and recognize what it would take to make the claim true.[2] But Foot has not completely ruled out the possibility of someone holding as a moral view that it is good to clasp one's hands in this fashion. She maintains rather that such a moral view would require a special background; in this case, the clasper's belief that such action has special significance or effect that pertains to the human good (VV 120). Foot contends that there is a logical impossibility in taking the clasping to be morally good *without* any such background. Hare apparently wants to insist that he can make sense of the goodness without the background Foot believes to be necessary—at which point, one wonders what could adjudicate this dispute. It seems to be a matter of conflicting linguistic intuitions, yet these are conflicting intuitions with important implications.

Does morality have only contingent connection with the human good, as Hare thinks, or a necessary one, as Foot believes? Let us look at the implications of the two conceptions of morality and take stock of the problems faced by each view. As we saw in the previous chapter, one advantage of Hare's concept of morality is that it preserves the connection between moral judgment and choice. Yet, this connection comes at a price—first, two rational individuals could hear all the evidence relevant to a moral judgment, and yet, still adhere to different judgments based on that evidence. This is because one is always free to choose different principles, so two individuals may diverge in their attitudes when faced with the same facts. Also, two people can count entirely different ranges of fact as evidence because those different ranges of fact are pertinent to the principles they each embrace.[3] Hence, moral judgment threatens to become arbitrary. Second, Hare preserves the connection between moral judgment and choice at the expense of losing touch with why morality is important—its connection with the human good. This point has a somewhat paradoxical air; after all, it seems that preserving the connection with choice implies that moral judgments, as Hare understands them, are necessarily important. It may be that the hand clasper believes his actions to be significant; however, this activity has no connection with what anyone else would regard as important, and it is surely the connection with the human good that gives morality its importance.

To these first two points, Hare has some rebuttal. He argues that there is an evolutionary story to be told as to why we do not make the absurd choices in Foot's examples and why our choices tend to promote the human good. According to Hare, to follow the example set by the hand clasper:

> . . . would hardly contribute to our growth, survival, procreation, etc.; if there have been any races of men or animals who have made the clasping and unclasping of hands a prime object of their pro-attitudes, to the exclusion of other more survival promoting activities, they have gone under in the struggle for existence.[4]

Here, it appears as though Hare is making the connection with the human good that Foot advocates. Yet, there is a crucial difference—in Foot's view, there is a logical connection between moral concepts and human good and harm. By contrast, for Hare, the connection is merely contingent because it is an upshot of a weeding-out process that could have had a different outcome. Perhaps there is a group of hand-claspers who, while possessing the requisite survival mechanisms, care uniquely about hand clasping. It is perfectly imaginable that a mild obsession with hand clasping would not detract from the functionality of survival mechanisms that persist despite the claspers' indifference to them. Also, hand clasping need not be the exclusive object of their pro-attitudes for Foot's objection to have weight. We could imagine hand claspers who also care about their survival mechanisms, such as opposition to murder and theft.

Foot's view of morality faces two hurdles—first, she must show that there can be a logical connection between the facts about what is good and harmful to humans, on the one hand, and moral goodness and badness, on the other. Second, she must show that if there is such a logical connection between fact and value, there can still be some connection between moral views and choice. In other words, she runs the risk of purchasing a degree of objectivity and importance at the price of practical irrelevance. The concern is that if facts are at the foundation of moral judgment, we can stand back and contemplate them as idly as one can contemplate the craters on the moon, without being moved to act on them. In what follows, I will lay out Foot's arguments for the existence of logical connections between facts and evaluative judgments. Then, I will begin to address the issue of the practicality of factual–evaluative judgments. This topic is one on which Foot had two changes of position. I discuss her initial understanding in this chapter, and her first change of mind in the next.

From facts to values: Rudeness

In "Moral Arguments" (1958), Foot mounts a direct argument for the possibility of deriving evaluative conclusions from factual premises. She believes that the concept of rudeness is one that links facts and evaluation. According to her, rudeness is an evaluative concept because calling something "rude" expresses mild condemnation. Yet, it is also a concept with clear criteria of application; one cannot decide that an act was rude simply by reacting as one would to rude behavior. It is important to note here that the fact of having offended someone does not make that particular behavior rude; rather, to say that some action was rude designates that behavior as an instance of a kind that causes offence. Specifically, Foot defines rudeness as "the kind of behavior [that] causes offence by indicating lack of respect" (VV 102). Foot believes that when certain facts obtain, one can draw the conclusion that the behavior in question is rude. Some such facts are conventional (e.g., raising and displaying your middle finger to another) and some are naturally disrespectful (e.g., shoving someone out of your way). Foot's point here is that there are certain types of acts that indicate a lack of respect and are therefore rude. It is no objection that "indicating lack of respect" uses the term "respect," which appears to be a value term.[5] The issue is simply whether there are some facts that amount to indicating a lack of respect and therefore amount to being rude. Foot claims that there are, and therefore one can infer from such facts an act of rudeness. In other words, one can infer the evaluative proposition that something is rude from the factual premises that an offensive condition obtained.

There are two questions worth entertaining concerning this argument. First, does Foot really succeed in establishing that we infer an evaluative claim from a fact or set of facts in this case? Second, if she does, what ramifications does it have for the noncognitivist views she is addressing? In one of the very few careful discussions of Foot's rudeness argument, Anne Thomas argues that Foot does not succeed in establishing that her examples are cases of deducing values from facts.[6] She distinguishes two different senses in which one might be said to deduce values from facts in the case of rudeness:

(1) There is some description, D, of person or action, A, such that if D is true of A, we must condemn A for rudeness.
(2) There is some description, D, of person or action, A, such that if D is true of A, "A is rude" is also true.

Thomas holds that (2) differs from (1) in that (1) contains the deduction of an evaluation from a set of facts, whereas in (2), there is an evaluative statement that is deduced from the facts, and it is, in principle, possible for this evaluative statement to be used descriptively, that is, without using it to condemn someone. Thomas distinguishes a further possible logical connection between the description of facts and an evaluative statement:

(3) There is some description, D, of person or action A, such that if A is rude, then A is D.

In (1) and (2), the truth of D is regarded as a sufficient condition for deducing an evaluation or evaluative statement (E). To put the matter symbolically, both (1) and (2) say D ⊃ E. With (3), the descriptions are only a necessary condition for deeming something rude (E ⊃ D). Thomas holds that only (3) is true. Thomas asks—can we deny that someone has done something rude if they have knowingly done that which causes offence? The answer, she believes, is yes. She agrees with Foot that "rudeness" is a mildly condemnatory description; yet, she thinks we need not condemn someone for causing an offence. So, we might not want to call someone "rude" who has knowingly caused an offence, and this claim clearly goes against (1). But (2) also does not hold up because, Thomas argues, the statement "A is rude" is necessarily condemnatory. Therefore, despite initial appearances, it cannot be used without condemning someone. That is, we would not want to use the statement "A is rude" in circumstances where we do not hold that the offence merits condemnation. According to Thomas, neither of the first two statements holds true because there is no requirement to condemn someone for causing offence, and to use the word "rude" is to express condemnation. In the case of (3), it does not achieve what Foot is seeking—namely, the deduction of values from facts. Therefore, Thomas concludes, Foot's argument fails.

Foot has a possible reply here. One can say something condemnatory about another or about an action without expressing an overall condemnation of that person or deed. As Thomas acknowledges, the condemnatory sense of "rude" is operative even when we say things like "How deliciously rude that was!" In such a statement, we are actually praising someone for doing something rude, while simultaneously relishing the badness of what that person did. Such occurrences are perfectly possible and indeed commonplace. Therefore, as Foot and Thomas agree, the term "rude" is fundamentally condemnatory, and yet, one can still say that "A's action is rude" without condemning A or even his action. There is, however, an important difference between talking about actions, or "pieces of behavior," as Foot explicitly does in "Moral Arguments," and talking about a person's character. When we say that someone is F, we make the attribution of a global character trait. Hence, when I say "Jones is rude," I am indeed condemning him in the sense of making a globally negative judgment about his character, something I may wish to withhold from doing even if Jones has, in fact, done something rude. Actions can be assessed as rude without expressing an overall condemnation. For instance, if the only way I can keep a political activist from attending an event where an assassination attempt is to be made on his life is by brazenly insulting him and his cause, we can say that this action is clearly rude, but something which must be done all the same. It is rude, but not to be condemned for its rudeness. Even in such cases, "rude" is condemnatory. The action is, to that extent, bad but still to be done. Hence, I believe Foot does successfully defend (2) rewritten as:

(2*) There is some description, D, of action, A, such that if D is true of A, "A is rude" is also true.

Here, the troubling "person" is omitted. There are no legitimate qualifiers that apply to label a stretch of intentionally offensive behavior as rude, even if we do not want to condemn it overall. In this qualified way, Foot has shown that we can derive an evaluative statement from a set of facts.

The next question is—what does the rudeness argument establish? Of course, it establishes that in this case, one may derive an evaluative statement from a fact, and this might seem rather trivial. Nevertheless, Foot thinks that her argument has important philosophical consequences because, as she sees it, it debunks a presumption against the derivation of values from facts. Yet, as mentioned in the previous chapter, both Stevenson and Hare acknowledge the existence of virtue and vice terms. Virtue and vice terms are tied to specific facts, as they acknowledge, but they think that "good" and "right" are unlike virtue and vice terms in that the criteria for their application is distinct from their meaning. The criteria for applying such terms, according to these two philosophers, can vary without changing their meanings, and this indicates that the meaning of such terms is not tied to any facts. Hence, they might be willing to admit Foot's point, but would still argue against her that it has limited implications for morality.

Foot has a response to this point. In "When is a Principle a Moral Principle?" she argues that one cannot separate one's judgments of right and wrong from our vocabulary of virtues and vices. I discuss her argument for this point below. A deeper problem for Foot's argument is that she admits that one can resist the values contained in virtue and vice terms by simply avoiding the use of those terms. As Marvin Glass points out, this admission seems to saddle Foot with the precise problem for which she criticizes Stevenson and Hare, inasmuch as one can refuse to draw an evaluative conclusion from the relevant evidence by simply refusing to use a term.[7] The problem here is that Foot's case is incomplete—a complete case for naturalism along the lines Foot proposes in "Moral Arguments" and "Moral Beliefs" (1958) would defend at least some list of terms that are necessary to describe features of actions in terms of their relevance to human good and harm. If rudeness belongs in that vocabulary, it is because it picks out features of actions which are *pro tanto* harmful to humans. If one were to refuse to use this term and had no relevant replacement for it, that person would be subject to moral criticism for which there is definite evidence.

From facts to values: Pride and fear

"Moral Beliefs" contains Foot's main arguments for the idea of a content restriction on moral judgments; specifically, she argues for the idea that there are logical connections between moral judgments and human well-being. Her argument is an analogical one, as she begins by claiming that pride and fear have a connection with conditions that must obtain to be used intelligibly. She then argues that the term "good" is like both "pride" and "fear" in having limitations on its intelligible use. The analogy draws on the fact that the emotions of pride and fear are evaluative. Since to feel pride in something is to see it as an achievement, the object of pride is taken to be good. Likewise, because one fears something as threatening to do evil, to feel fear is to evaluate that thing as bad. These feelings evaluate their objects. Foot aims to show that one cannot intelligibly feel these emotions in relation to just any object; therefore, there are important logical connections between facts and values. Ultimately, she aims to show that evaluation and commendation, in general, only make sense in relation to certain kinds of objects.

Following Wittgenstein's *Philosophical Investigations*, Foot argues that to be said to be feeling certain emotions, it is not sufficient that one be in a certain mental state.[8] Rather, the person must stand in an appropriate relationship to a proper object of those feelings. Pride, for example, is not merely some feeling of elevation. She argues that it does not make sense to take pride in something that is not one's own achievement. For example, if I thought I had been awarded the prize for best pumpkin and felt proud of this triumph, but it turned out that it was, in fact, someone else's pumpkin that actually won, I could not intelligibly continue to feel pride. Further, what one takes pride in must be some sort of achievement or advantage. It would not make sense to feel pride in laying one hand over another three times in an hour, unless there is a special background condition, such as a stroke, which made this a difficult task and an important step in recovery. Similarly, feeling fear is more than merely turning pale and trembling; one must have these reactions in response to something believed to be of a threatening evil. In this way, Foot attempts to show that "even feelings are logically vulnerable to facts" (VV 115).

She recognizes that her noncognitivist opponents will have an immediate objection to these claims. They could acknowledge her points, and yet say that what counts as an achievement or an evil is a matter of individual attitude (VV 116). In response to this objection, Foot discusses the concept of danger and its connection with injury. She believes that something can be considered a danger only through threatening bodily injury, and that there are specific objective conditions that limit what can be regarded as such. Specifically, a body part is injured when it is impaired from fulfilling its function; Foot argues that this connection between injury and function narrowly limits what can count as an injury. As she points out, a body part's basic function is not the only way it can be used; a court jester may use his ears to entertain, but that is not the function of ears (VV 117). The function of ears relates to general features of the human condition, rather than the special and unique ways an individual can make use of them. At the furthest limit, someone may be said to be injured if one's body were altered to such an extent that one experienced lasting pain, though without impairment to function. To fear that one may be injured is to believe, then, that there is some threat of such a state being inflicted by something.

The point of this stretch of argument is to show that only certain kinds of beliefs will license one to say "I am afraid." One must believe that there is a danger, and to believe that there is danger, one must, in turn, believe that there is a threat of bodily injury. Of course, one can believe that there is a threat of bodily injury in unusual circumstances, and hence there can be eccentric fears. Yet, Foot has still connected the feeling of fear to facts about the world that one must believe obtain in order to be said to feel fear. Fear, then, is more than a particular inner state, but is connected with a specific range of objects, namely, those that threaten bodily injury.

Unfortunately, Foot seems to be mistaken in many of her claims regarding pride and fear. First, one can clearly feel proud of something that is not one's own achievement. People often feel pride over the victory of a local team or of their nation during times of war, even though the achievement in question was in no way under their control.[9] Such people *may* believe that their support, even their silent mental support, played some occult role in the victory, but this does not seem necessary for the intelligible attribution of pride to them. Of course, Foot acknowledges that people can identify with others and thereby take pride in another's achievement, and perhaps this idea could provide her some sort of rebuttal. Yet, the mechanism of this identification is hazy, and it is unclear what sort of constraints there may be on the application of pride if we admit such identification. Further, in the case of fear, one can clearly feel fear standing on the edge of a precipice even though there is no real danger of falling off; such a fear need not be the result of a false belief that one will fall off the edge. It is a case of "recalcitrant emotion," in which an emotion persists in spite of a firm belief that should have neutralized the emotion.[10] As Justin D'Arms and Daniel Jacobson point out, Foot cannot simply attribute a belief in danger in view of the fact that an agent is afraid because this would trivialize the view.[11] She intends, after all, to set out the conditions on the intelligible attribution of fear, and such a view would not allow for any limitations. However, surely there are some conceptual limitations, even if Foot has not gotten them right. Consider a man standing in a skyscraper's top-floor viewing area looking down, through clear glass windows, onto the city street far below. What makes his rapid pulse, sweatiness, and other symptoms a fear-reaction, even though he fully realizes that he is safely behind a barrier and probably safer than if he were standing on the city street far below? Need he have thoughts of bodily harm, as Foot argues, or is it sufficient that we (the appraisers) can intelligibly connect his response to bodily harm in similar situations, that is, situations of standing precariously on a cliff? The latter seems to be correct, and this connection is much less restricted than Foot's requirements; anything that we can connect to a similar situation that posed a threat of danger seems to underwrite our attribution of fear. The fear of heights is so common that we readily recognize fear in such a situation, but the psychoanalytic tradition reveals that some connections can be highly idiosyncratic; we can make some bizarre responses intelligible by looking at individual histories. Further, the connection can be evolutionary, in that possessing a phobia of heights, snakes, and insects may make some evolutionary sense, even if the response is out of proportion with what is considered a genuine danger. If this claim is correct, there is a set of symptoms that enables us to identify a response as fearful, and these symptoms bear a causal connection to past situations in which there was a threat of bodily harm—a connection that can be unique to the individual or part of the shared human history.

The counterexamples to Foot's claims support a noncognitivist view of the emotions, which denies that emotions are defined by judgments, and these counterexamples appear to damage the case Foot was attempting to build in "Moral Beliefs." But is her case damaged beyond repair? Perhaps not; after all, she is surely correct about the pumpkin grower who, at least, cannot intelligibly continue to feel pride having discovered that the prize-winning pumpkin belonged to someone else. Feeling pride over one's prize-winning pumpkin depends on the belief, among many others one must possess, that one has indeed grown the prize-winning pumpkin and the true belief that this is some sort of achievement. Some fears, similarly, are joined to judgments; the fear that the stock market will plunge, for example, requires a belief on the part of the fearful person that the market may plummet. These facts exclude many nonhuman animals from having such emotions, although we can attribute to them the more basic fears. Many nonbasic emotions, however, are subject to refutation by relevant facts, and so the question then becomes whether or not moral concepts are like those nonbasic feelings. Moral judgments do seem to require rather sophisticated assessments; they require certain beliefs about their objects, and must be withdrawn if those beliefs are demonstrably false. Moral judgments and their associated sentiments, therefore, seem more like such nonbasic emotions than like the basic emotions that cause trouble for Foot, though she does not provide this bit of argument. As noted above, Foot thinks the hand clasper who sees his action as good in some moral sense would have to believe that his actions fulfilled a duty or was, in some way, virtuous (VV 119). In either case, there are limits; one cannot have a duty to do just anything. In the case of virtues such as courage, the action in question must be done for the sake of some real or imagined usefulness. Without some special background, the action of clasping hands cannot be considered courageous or charitable. It is hard to see under what sort of circumstances one could have a duty to clasp one's hands three times in an hour; surely such a context could be conjured, but the specificity of the circumstances is what lend force to Foot's claim that there are logical limits to the application of a concept like "good." In this way, Foot's argument can be revised to show that making moral judgments is like feeling pride and some nonbasic instances of fear in that they are essentially related to certain factual judgments. Suitably qualified, then, her argument has some force.

Naturalism and the virtues

It is interesting to juxtapose the argument of Foot's "Moral Beliefs" with a complementary argument made in her earlier article "When Is a Principle a Moral Principle?" There, she makes the surprising claim that in order to justify the judgment that a newly discovered culture has the view that stealing is wrong, it would not be sufficient to find out that they make consistent choices falling under general rules that forbid taking things acknowledged by them as another's personal property. Instead, we have to picture them as using a set of more specific descriptions of the actions and having reactions that correspond to those descriptions. As Foot puts it:

> I am arguing that . . . it is only against a background of thoughts about stealing – ways of looking at it – that we can use these

words [viz., 'they believe stealing is wrong']. And it does not make sense to say that they may see it like this or like that if they do not describe such things, and do not express specific reactions, as we do when we speak of treachery, cunning, or cruelty. (WPMP 109)

Here, Foot is arguing that rules that capture feelings of approval and disapproval toward a type of action do not constitute moral principles. Rather, there is a family of more specific descriptions and reactions that we must connect with general principles in order to attribute a genuine moral principle to someone. Though she is not explicit about why those more specific reactions are required, it seems that they capture the variety of responses of one who cares about the human good. In other words, we do not merely approve of actions that fall under a moral rule and disapprove of actions that do not; instead the possession of moral principles is a matter of having a response with a specific valence in view of an action's impact on human well-being. For example, we revile the treachery in someone who cunningly cheats another out of his inheritance in view of all that the legatee could have done for his family. Without that connection to human weal or woe, our various responses would not make sense. Foot's complaint here is that Hare has rested the approval and disapproval entirely in the appraiser's attitudes, severing those responses from what they are about.

Also in this article, she challenges the idea that there is a single underlying evaluative meaning. She argues that there are as many evaluative meanings as there are disparate reactions; to say that something is "treacherous" differs from saying that same thing is "cruel." Surely they are both negative evaluations, but, she thinks, they express diverse evaluative responses based on different dispositions evinced by the actions in relation to human well-being. Vices such as treachery and cruelty are distinct characteristics that we condemn in different ways—the cruel person can inflict suffering with enjoyment, and a treacherous person willingly plots evil for her own gain. An action can be treacherous and cruel, or only one of them, and in each case, our response, though negative, would differ; for example, we typically experience horror at someone's cruelty, while we feel outrage at someone's treachery. Even here, our responses are subject to fine, contextual features of individual situations. She thereby disputes Hare's thesis, described in Chapter 1, that these terms share a common evaluative meaning with differing descriptive criteria.

We can see that in this trio of early articles, "When Is a Principle a Moral Principle?," "Moral Arguments," and "Moral Beliefs," Foot begins to make a case for a naturalistic ethics in which the virtues play a central role, and in which a trait is justified as a virtue by making a contribution to a good human life. So far, this case is only outlined, but more detail will be laid out in her later works, which will be addressed in Chapters 4–6. Her case for such an ethics is motivated by metaethical concerns, specifically her dissatisfaction regarding the ability of noncognitivist theories to offer an adequate account of morality. In Foot's view, the virtues are essential to having a moral outlook inasmuch as they bridge our various moral responses to the human good. More explicitly, the virtues perform three functions for her. First, they provide a descriptive vocabulary that captures the motivational dispositions of persons with respect to human weal and woe. That is, they describe various ways in which persons may successfully or unsuccessfully register the impact of their actions on human well-being. Second, they track various morally salient aspects of actions. That is, they track features of actions that have an impact on human weal and woe. Third, they express various reactions with regard to those morally salient aspects of actions. They fulfill all of these functions within the context of a factual connection to the human good. However, Foot is careful to point out that this connection can be rather loose; courage is not, she believes, necessarily connected with saving lives, but a courageous action must be done for the sake of something worthwhile.[12] Our reaction to an act of cowardice is a moral one because we disapprove of the action, and therefore the agent, in their failure to bring about some good, where goodness is defined in relation to human well-being. Hence, our descriptions of actions are susceptible to challenge by facts regarding whether what we take to be good for human beings is indeed so.[13] At this point, she argues that virtues must provide reasons for each individual to act by somehow being in their self-interest. She agrees with Plato that justice must be good for the just man (VV 126). She thus advocates a eudaemonist view of the virtues, which is the view that the virtues must benefit their possessors, and this is because she holds that the virtues must benefit their possessors if there is to be any reason for individuals to act virtuously.[14] Yet, this is a difficult position to maintain in view of the fact that virtues, such as justice, often demand that we make significant sacrifices. As we will see in the next chapter, this consideration leads her to abandon eudaemonism. Up to this point, Foot has only defended the possibility of a moral theory with such a foundation against some of the reasons it had been thought to be impossible. Nevertheless, even this small step is an important contribution.

Does Foot's naturalistic ethics fall to the open question argument? When framed to address her view, it would ask "that [trait or action] may promote human well-being, but is it good?" For Foot, this question is indeed as nonsensical as asking "he may be a never-married adult male, but is he a bachelor?" These two things are identical in her view, and so, the question does not sound open to her, but rather tautological, and therefore for her, the argument has no weight. Still, one might question whether she has really captured the meaning of goodness, on three separate grounds—first, as Hare pointed out, the naturalist will seem to have difficulty commending if goodness simply means "promoting human well-being." After all, to describe something as promoting well-being is different from praising it. Yet, one need not have a special vocabulary to commend; an existing vocabulary of goodness together with the virtues, sometimes used with emphasis and in a special context, can do the job satisfactorily. Second, there is the concern raised by Hare that Foot commits herself to dogmatic conventionalism by tying moral terms to specific content. Hare seems to think that if naturalism is true, we cannot criticize the norms of a society; if our moral vocabulary is indeed tied to specific descriptive content, we could not intelligibly say that we should do otherwise than what our society recommends. Hare thinks that only if we can separate the meaning and criteria of moral terms (at least for terms such as "right" and "wrong," and "good" and "bad") can we apply these terms in opposition to the usage of our society. That is, we can commend actions that our fellows condemn or vice versa because the commendatory and condemnatory meaning of "good" and "bad" is not attached to specific content. Therefore, Hare believes his noncognitivist view to be superior to Foot's naturalism. Yet, there are three problems with Hare's objection. First, let us say that someone lights upon the correct naturalistic definition, that "good" in at least one sense means "promoting human well-being," for example. It could be that society at large does not embrace the correct analysis; Hare simply assumes that the analysis would cash out exactly the current use of our society, but it could be that the correct analysis is revisionary. After all, our usage is surely not uniform. Alternatively, against the apparent facts, it could be that our society *does* use "good" in exactly the right way. In that case, there is no need for opposition to that definition, and the only remaining questions will be about factual matters concerning what actually promotes well-being. Hare seems not to have considered these possibilities in framing this objection. Second, Hare's criticism assumes a naturalism that is much more simplistic than Foot's version. Foot's conception of human well-being is not explicitly spelled out, but it is clear that this is no simple notion. Indeed, "When Is a Principle a Moral Principle?" makes clear that her conception of the meaning of moral concepts is holistic, in that the meaning of "good" and "bad" depend on the connections we make with other concepts such as "honesty," "sincerity," "murder," "stealing," and "treachery" (WPMP 108). As she writes, "Concepts of this [latter] kind enable a man to connect new, possibly surprising applications of 'good' or 'bad' with one particular set of other cases – to say, e.g., that wearing bright colors is bad in the same way as boasting" (Ibid.). This passage suggests that virtue and vice terms, along with other evaluative action descriptions, help us spell out our conception of a good human life; they do not neatly resolve themselves into nonevaluative definitions.

The third problem with Hare's objection lies in the meaning of terms such as "honesty" and "courage," which need not be fixed to particular descriptive content under naturalism. Foot does not make this point herself, but rather, it comes from Iris Murdoch, who describes a response to Hare for a naturalist such as Foot. Murdoch writes, "We have a different image of courage at forty from that which we had at twenty. A deepening process, at any rate an altering and complicating process, takes place."[15] This process is not simply a matter of applying commendation to a different range of descriptive content, but rather, it means having a deeper understanding of which behaviors merit being described as courageous. One might realize that what one once thought to be cantankerous, mean-spirited behavior was actually motivated by sincere devotion to a cause. If someone risks being viewed as nasty for the sake of standing up to his opponents, he may merit being called "courageous." In such ways, evaluative terms can be used to revise other such terms, as well as to sharpen our overall conception of the good human life. Hence, Hare is wrong to think that naturalism necessarily results in a rigid adherence to convention; there is plenty of room for the development of revisionary moral judgments within naturalistic views such as Foot advocates, provided the judgments maintain some connection with the human good. Finally, there is the concern that Foot has not shown us how "good," in the sense she describes, connects to choices, and so it seems that something is missing from her conception of good that is indeed connected to our use of good.

Moral concepts and reasons for action

Noncognitivists believed they had revived a crucial idea from David Hume, who argued that moral concepts have a necessary connection to the will, which is our capacity for making choices.[16] For Hare, all evaluative concepts have a necessary connection with choice. When I apply an evaluative concept such as "good" to some class of thing, I commit myself to choosing that particular class, at least under the relevant circumstances. So, when I say sincerely, "That is an excellent fishing rod," I indicate that it is the sort of fishing rod I would choose if I were going fishing and in need of a new rod. As Hare would put it, I commit myself to an imperatival principle of the form "Let me choose such rods." In "Goodness and Choice" (1961), Foot argues that the commitment to choice is neither necessary nor sufficient for correctly applying the term "good" to anything; choice itself is not sufficient to make something good because things may not be good in spite of the fact that I would choose them. She argues that someone's choice of rusty knives does not intelligibly make the knives good, even for that person; he simply chooses poorly, assuming that he has the possibility of getting some sharp, noncorroded knives. Some classes of things (e.g., knives) have functions that fix criteria for goodness, and there are also roles that fix criteria for goodness, such as "farmer" and "liar." Moreover, there are criteria for the goodness of things such as coal and art, which are determined by their customary use or the kind of interest we take in them. Of course, an individual's undertakings can create circumstances that allow for idiosyncratic uses of "good," but this is a qualified sense of goodness—"good for his purposes" or "good from his point of view" (VV 140). Likewise, choice is not necessary for goodness. Certain things may be good even though I may never be in the position to choose them, as good tree roots contribute to the life of an organism and my choices are irrelevant to their goodness (VV 133, 145). As she puts it, "only someone in the grip of a theory would insist that when we speak of a good root we commit ourselves in some way to choosing a root like that" (VV 145).[17]

Foot thereby completely rejects the sort of connection between evaluative concepts and the will, as advocated by Hare. Still, she accepts that moral concepts, including some applications of "good" to actions and persons, give each individual reason to choose those actions and to become a certain kind of person, and she does this despite rejecting the view that these terms express the attitudes of the individual. To answer Hare, she must offer some alternative view of the necessary connection that she posits between moral concepts and the will, according to which, anyone who sincerely judges that certain actions or dispositions are morally good will then choose them. She makes this argument in the second part of "Moral Beliefs." In the view she advocates there, anyone has reason to cultivate the virtues, even if they lack the desire to do so at a given moment.[18] Further, because everyone has reason to cultivate the virtues, everyone has reason to act virtuously. Foot's early view is therefore a version of moral rationalism—the view that moral facts necessarily provide reasons for rational agents.

Her view in "Moral Beliefs" is that there is a connection between virtue and self-interests, where virtues are something every rational agent must want because they are essentially beneficial to their possessor. This view is a version of eudaemonism—the general thesis that virtues benefit their possessors. In "Moral Beliefs," Foot takes it to be uncontroversial that rational agents will take anything that is in their own interests to give them reason to act, and she then aims to show that cultivating virtues is always in one's interest, and failing to do so is necessarily against one's interest. She thereby claims to show that we each have reason to cultivate virtues. In the course of her argument, she attempts to refute the position advocated by Thrasymachus in Plato's *Republic*—namely, the view that it is more profitable to be unjust, a view which she calls "Thrasymachus' thesis" (VV 125). So, she aims to persuade us that justice, along with the other so-called "cardinal virtues" of courage, prudence, and temperance are, in some sense, profitable in spite of the fact that these virtues may at times ask us to make drastic sacrifices, even to the degree of laying down our lives.

Foot's early eudaemonist moral rationalism has, I think, been widely misunderstood due to lack of attention to the details of her highly condensed argument. One such detail is the somewhat unusual view of reasons for action that she takes here, which is derived from Anscombe's treatment of the philosophy of action in *Intention*. A theory of reasons for action tells us what it is to provide a reason that can do things such as motivate or justify an action. One of the default positions is that a reason for action is a true belief that doing some action will satisfy some desire we have. In her early work, Foot does not subscribe to this view, at least on a certain understanding of it. Anscombe's view is that satisfying a desire does not automatically provide a reason; stating "I just want it" does not provide a reason for getting a twig of mountain ash.[19] Someone may feel inexplicably compelled to get a twig of mountain ash, but that compulsion is not a reason, according to this view. To want something only qualifies as a reason when that which is desired has some apparent goodness to the person with the desire. Yet, there are various ways in which something can be good, according to Anscombe. There are various characteristics that can give me a reason to act by giving the action the appearance of achieving something good; some of the examples given by Anscombe include being pleasant, fun, digestible and wholesome, being something one should do, or being appropriate for the kind of person one is. Despite the central role of goodness in Anscombe's view, she insists that she is not giving us a morally loaded theory of reasons; one of the examples she uses involves a doomed Nazi who believes it fitting to spend his waning minutes killing Jews.[20] The Nazi really does possess such reasons, though we find his reasoning and actions morally despicable. Nevertheless, she insists that the good ascribed to something must truly belong to one of the many forms of "good" in order for it to be a genuine reason for action. Hence, there is some formal constraint on reasons, in Anscombe's view.

Foot borrows from Anscombe the notion that a variety of desirability characteristics can give reasons for action. As Foot points out, no one needs to give a reason as to why he does not want to be bored or why he wishes to pursue his interests; the descriptions themselves give reasons. That moral descriptions give reasons requires proof, she thinks, and it does not follow from the concept of morality that moral descriptions provide us with reasons. We cannot assume that the term "unjust" gives a description of a possible action that satisfactorily terminates an inquiry into the reasons not to perform that action. The most obvious way to show that it does, Foot evidently thinks, is to demonstrate that it is always in every person's interest to be just and to avoid injustice. In that case, there is a necessary connection between being just and fulfilling one's own interests; hence, the fact that some action is just will always give a reason to do it. Yet, it is important to note that the inquiry into whether it is always in one's interest to be just is not, at least for Foot, part of an even deeper inquiry demonstrating that being just maximizes pleasure or the satisfaction of our desires. Pleasure is just a different sort of desirability characteristic, according to the view as adopted from Anscombe, and Foot does not accept this as a definition of what is in our own best interest. Maximizing the fulfillment of our desires also does not serve as an adequate description, since not every desire is for something even apparently good.

Foot's case for seeing the virtues as giving us reasons is, in part, an argument by analogy; specifically, she wants to compare injustice with physical injury, focusing primarily on an injury to our limbs. She believes that an injury is something we each have *pro tanto* reason to want to avoid. That is, we want to avoid it for itself, even though some circumstance may arise where there is a reason to want to sustain an injury because of some advantage that can be realized through it (or, more commonly, we want to do something that *risks* sustaining injury for the sake of some advantage). In such circumstances, we can say that there are overriding, or all things considered, reasons to sustain or risk an injury, but clearly we would avoid the injury if the gain could be realized without sustaining it. No rational person seeks an injury for itself, and every rational person avoids injury for itself. An injury is something that we should always want to avoid because it is a physical change that impairs the function of a particular body part, and we all have reason to want our bodies to function properly (VV 116–17; VV 122). We all have reason to want our bodies to function properly because having a properly functioning body is an all-purpose means for achieving nearly anything one may want. As Foot illustrates this point:

> Hands and eyes, like ears and legs, play a part in so many operations that a man could only be said not to need them if he had no wants at all. That such people exist, in asylums, is not to the present purpose at all; the proper use of his limbs is something a man has reason to want if he wants anything. (VV 122)

Here, she makes a specific claim that intact limbs are something that every rational person wants. It is worth focusing on the details of this intriguing claim, for it is the core of Foot's argument regarding the necessary reason-giving force of moral reasons.

Foot believes that injury to our limbs is something that we all have reason to avoid because the use of our limbs is something which "a man has reason to want if he wants anything" (122). This makes the possession of limbs sound similar to a natural primary good in John Rawls' sense, according to which these natural properties, such as abilities, talents, and health, normally have a use for people, whatever sort of life they choose.[21] Yet, while Rawls thinks we may simply "presume" rational people want such primary goods, Foot is quite clear that she thinks it *necessary* that all rational agents want them. She is not, however, simply defining rationality so that only those who want their limbs can be counted as rational.

General facts concerning human beings support the idea that it is necessary for rational people to want their limbs intact. The point being made here by Foot is not that it is a general fact that everyone happens to want something for which the possession of intact limbs would be advantageous. Rather, the point is that the conditions of human life are such that wanting intact limbs is rationally necessary. As Anscombe pointed out, the primitive sign of wanting is "trying to get."[22] Given the basic physical facts of human existence, the act of 'trying to get' requires reaching out in some way. Therefore, according to both Foot and Anscombe, everyone must want intact limbs because they will be beneficial to everyday human life, which is characterized by wants and certain typical ways of attaining them. Wanting various things is surely a universal and constant feature of human life, with limbs playing a rather special role in the fulfilling of those desires. For Foot, wanting our limbs intact is a special case of wanting; it is tied intimately to my desire for other things, and it is this connection that gives the relation between wanting intact limbs and wanting other things a necessity that is lacking in other cases. Nevertheless, the connection between wanting one's limbs intact and wanting other things is not a typical means–end relation. Limbs, as Foot clearly sees, are not the exclusive way for us to achieve our wants; yet, they are also not merely a tool that can be picked up and put away for certain purposes. Rather, the possession of healthy limbs is typically necessary to the execution of my wants, even if I now happen to have other means, such as a fleet of responsive servants, at my disposal to fulfill individual wants. As Foot recognizes, someone may object by pointing to the possibility of an individual who could foresee never having an occasion to need use of his limbs: for example, because he will have servants throughout his life who will substitute for his own hands and eyes (VV 123). However, because no one can be in a position that foresees that such circumstances can be maintained throughout one's life, Foot believes this objection fails. When I deny that I want my limbs intact, I am not necessarily denying that I want the indispensable means to achieve some other want, which is often called "instrumental irrationality." I may be failing to choose the indispensable means to what I want, but even when I am not, I am denying my want for something that is centrally involved in the execution of my wants generally, and Foot sees that denial as being irrational. Hence, Foot's argument for the rational necessity of wanting our limbs is tied to objective features of the human condition, specifically that limbs, which are (at present) irreplaceable if lost, are normally essential to the execution of one's will and the fulfillment of desires. She is not staking her claim on the fact that people generally possess the desire to preserve their limbs.

Similarly, she thinks that there are features of human life that explain why it is rationally necessary for us to want the virtues. Yet, how far does this analogy extend? Can the virtues be taken to be as essential to the fulfillment of our desires as are our limbs? Foot seems to believe so, although she only sketches this line of thought in the concluding paragraphs of "Moral Beliefs," where she addresses the rationality of choosing to be just. There are additional facts about the human form of life that are relevant here; specifically, our inevitably social nature. Though we may choose to live a life in isolation, or indeed though we may be stranded in involuntary isolation due to transportation malfunctions or international nuclear aggressions, we are creatures who can, at present, anticipate that our attempts at attaining things will happen in a social environment. This means that we are creatures for whom it is a constant fact that our attempts at achieving a particular want may be interfered with or enhanced by others.

The basic idea behind Foot's defense of justice is this—we will all profit if our actions instance a practice defined by mutual respect and fidelity to promises, and this profit is one we all must want, given that our desiring things predictably occurs within a social matrix. Foot addresses possible counterexamples, including those involving cases of the strong and powerful. It may appear that people with such traits could avoid the costs of justice without sacrificing its benefits as they have the potential to coerce people into performing to their will or achieving their desires without the help of others. Foot does not consider the case of the brazenly unjust in her piece, perhaps because she thinks it obvious that it is covered by the same reply that she gave in the case of the man who supposedly could make do without limbs—one simply cannot be assured that the conditions allowing one to live that way will persist. The tides may always turn against oppressive tyrants who will then pay the price for their unjust acts. She explicitly, though still very briefly, addresses the case of those who give lip service to justice while behaving unjustly. To receive the benefits of justice, they must conceal themselves from others. As she states:

> Philosophers often speak as if a man could thus hide himself even from those around him, but the supposition is doubtful, and in any case the price in vigilance would be colossal. If he lets even a few people see his true attitude he must guard himself against them; if he lets no one into the secret he must always be careful in case the least spontaneity betray him. Such facts are important because the need a man has for justice in dealings with other men depends on the fact that they are men and not inanimate objects or animals. (VV 129)

Here again, Foot argues from general facts regarding human life, and again, the point is not to justify the virtues as instrumentally necessary in the usual sense. Just as someone without limbs may get what he wants through fortunate circumstances, one's desires may be realized even though one is unjust. Still, as a rational agent, I must want justice, inasmuch as I want to reliably get the object of my desires without interference from other agents, and under conditions that I can reasonably expect to face. Justice may require me to forgo opportunities to acquire things, and it may ask of me to perform tasks that are costly in terms of the required time and effort. Yet, what is gained through surrendering these possible benefits and accepting the burdens of justice is an ability to strive for one's desires within such constraints, with a claim on either the cooperation or the noninterference of others. As stated by Anscombe in her paper "Promising and Its Justice" — "Getting people to do things without the application of physical force is a necessity for human life."[23] The completed analogy Foot wants to illustrate is—for fragile, social creatures of roughly matched power, justice is as central to our lives as are our limbs. And the conclusion she wishes us to draw is that no one can rationally lack the desire for justice.

Foot recognized one of the most obvious objections to this position, which is that of the "tight corner." That is, while it may be generally beneficial to be just or courageous, surely in individual circumstances, it is difficult to claim that someone has reason to be virtuous when, in doing so, they would incur a very great loss. With this objection, it would seem rational to avoid developing the disposition to be just in order to avoid incurring these losses. Foot herself seems to have found such an argument from the "tight corner" persuasive since she cites it as a reason for her change of view in "Morality as a System of Hypothetical Imperatives" (VV xv). Yet, there is arguably more to be said for her early eudaemonist views than she recognized. Ultimately, the successful defense of her early position depends on defending the view that we should not be focusing on the rationality of individual actions, but rather on the rationality of adopting the disposition to be just.

Although Foot did not explicitly carry out such a defense, Mark LeBar and Michael Thompson have treated this aspect of eudaemonism recently.[24] The core of this account is what Thompson calls a "two-level theory of rationality."[25] In such a theory, the rationality of individual just actions is a function of the rationality of a higher order practice or disposition that they express or embody. Such theories have two essential components—a transfer principle, which connects the rationality of individual actions to the rationality of the disposition they express, and a standard of appraisal, which tells us when the disposition itself is a rational one. In the view advocated by Foot, the transfer principle states that the rationality of the disposition to be just makes any action that expresses that disposition rational, and the standard of appraisal states that those dispositions are rational which promote the agent's self-interest. Foot directs her efforts in "Moral Beliefs" to proving that justice meets the standard of appraisal, but she does not spend any time defending the transfer principle, which seems to be the source of many complaints raised against her view. How is such a principle to be defended? It cannot be defended by appealing to the moral merit or the profitability of adhering to such a principle, for that would conflate the transfer principle with the standard of appraisal.[26] The transfer principle should be a formal one, not tied to a particular standard of appraisal. Whenever we attribute justice to an action, we are, in fact, appealing to such a principle. Each just act shares something in embodying or expressing the virtue of justice. The commonality of such acts derives from seeing them as instances acting from a disposition defined in terms of responding to a certain set of reasons. In the case of just actions, we may, for example, be responding to reasons to return some loaned item to its owner. The disposition to be responsive to such reasons can be embodied in multiple acts of a single agent and by the acts of any other appropriately circumstanced agent. All of those acts are to be understood by reference to the virtue of justice, which is a disposition to take certain reasons as reasons for action; to be just, or at least to employ a conception of justice, is to have mastery of a certain conception of rationality. To help us see that, Thompson points out that returning a borrowed book is both a just act and, from the perspective of a just agent, a rational act. Returning some autumn leaves that have blown into one's yard from a neighbor's yard is neither of these, even if the person returning them has similar occurrent thoughts when returning the leaves as when returning the book (e.g., "they are hers, therefore I must give them back").[27] The rationality of the disposition is conferred to the individual act that expresses it, and any act which is thought to be irrational cannot, therefore, be deemed an expression of that disposition. This illustrates that we operate with such a transfer principle; however, we assess the dispositions which we hold to make our actions rational. It could be that we are wrong in thinking that it is rational to attempt to become just, but we do employ such transfer principles in describing each other and ourselves as agents in a wide variety of contexts. The ability to engage in practices such as keeping promises requires us to develop dispositions to respond to reasons such as those that prompt us to return borrowed possessions, and this ability is a basic aspect of our agency; one can say this, I believe, without foreclosing the question of whether it is ultimately rational to be just or to keep one's promises.

What this suggests is that if justice meets a relevant standard of appraisal, then the rationality of acting justly in the "tight corner" cases is answered by appeal to the rationality of the disposition. The person who accepts this justification, and successfully develops the disposition to be just in light of it, would then no longer refer to that reasoning when called to explain his individual actions. He would then make appeal to reasons of justice because he would have come to see his self-interest in terms of being just.[28] We must take seriously the thought, emphasized by Mark LeBar and John McDowell, that in adopting such dispositions, one is adopting a new evaluative perspective. That is, the supposed sacrifice being made in the "tight corner" cases appears quite different to the just person than to someone who is not employing the concept of justice. The virtuous agent comes to see the value of acting justly, perhaps to such an extent that he sees intrinsic benefits to acting in such a manner, even in circumstances in which doing so comes with some terrible consequences.[29]

Foot's eudaemonist moral rationalism is still a viable position, despite the fact that she came to reject the position. It should be noted that her position here is neither a version of rational egoism, according to which the only reasons we have are reasons of self-interest, nor a version of ethical egoism, according to which the only moral obligation we have is to promote our self-interest. There are reasons for action that do not relate to self-interest, for Foot; it is just that in "Moral Beliefs," she believes self-interest to be the most promising route to demonstrating that moral reasons are genuine reasons. Eudaemonism should not be regarded as a version of ethical egoism because it justifies genuine moral obligations to others; reasons of self-interest are reasons to develop a disposition of justice. Reasons of justice are genuine reasons that require us to respect the interests of others; eudaemonism shows that the disposition to perform such acts is in the interest of the agent, not that the fulfillment of every obligation will be.

Although this hardly exhausts the range of problems one could raise for Foot's early account of the relation of moral concepts to choice, it does address some of the central issues. It suggests that this account is more defensible than it has been held to be, even by some of Foot's sympathetic readers, and perhaps even by Foot herself in her later writings. In the next chapter, I describe Foot's first change of mind on this issue, as set out in one of her most celebrated and widely discussed articles, "Morality as a System of Hypothetical Imperatives."

CHAPTER THREE

Against moral rationalism

"Considerations of justice, charity and the like have a strange and powerful appeal to the human heart, and we do not need bad arguments to show that no one could be indifferent to morality without error." (VV 156)

Reasons for action

Is someone who does something immoral necessarily irrational? According to Foot's position in "Moral Beliefs," the answer is "yes," as everyone who acts immorally fails to act by the set of dispositions that would best promote her own self-interest. However, Foot later began to have doubts about this position and eventually reversed her argument altogether, embracing the view that one could act immorally and still be rational. The view that a rational agent can act immorally is a version of a position called "externalism," according to which morality provides an agent with reason to act only in the presence of the agent's desire to be moral. Foot embraces externalism in "Morality as a System of Hypothetical Imperatives," rejecting her earlier view that any rational agent has reason to be moral. The reasons for this shift in position are unclear, but she indicates dissatisfaction with her earlier idea of appealing to the rationality of dispositions to vindicate the rationality of individual virtuous actions when those actions require significant sacrifice (VV xv). Foot also suggests that she simply never fully explored the idea that moral judgments may not always give reasons to every individual, simply because she was influenced by emotivism and prescriptivism (VV xv).

Yet, there is evidently a deeper philosophical context to her change of view. Between "Moral Beliefs" and "Morality as a System of Hypothetical Imperatives," Foot clearly alters her views about reasons for action from a theory inspired by Anscombe to one inspired by Hume, and it is important to recognize the differences between these views. As noted in Chapter 2, in her early work, Foot embraces Anscombe's view that a variety of desirability characteristics are automatically reason-giving (VV 127). We do not need to give a reason for avoiding boredom or pursuing pleasure or doing something that is manifestly in our best interest, but Foot does not think at this point in the development of her thought that we can assume without argument that "morally good action" is a description that gives sufficient justification for a practical decision. We have reason to do what is morally good because whatever falls under that description serves our self-interest, which is automatically reason-giving. In her middle period articles, "Reasons for Action and Desires" (1972) and "Morality as a System of Hypothetical Imperatives," (1972) Foot does not relinquish the idea that self-interest is automatically reason-giving, but she does hold that all other reasons for action depend on possessing relevant desires for their reason-giving force. She also rejects the idea that moral reasons can be shown to be genuine reasons through being shown to serve self-interest. Hence, she concludes that the reason-giving force of moral considerations depends on the possession of relevant desires by morally good agents, and whether we possess such desires is a contingent fact about us. Of course, it might be that each one of us has such desires, but Foot apparently believes this is not so.

Foot never held the view that considerations of self-interest would automatically move someone to act. Although she does not explicitly deny that view, it is quite implausible. Obviously, agents sometimes fail to pursue their self-interest, especially when under the influence of conditions such as depression. So, charity demands not saddling Foot with this view. Her view, in both her early and middle periods, is that considerations of self-interest are always genuine reasons, which will move rational agents to act because being rational requires having certain desires, such as the desire to do what is in one's interest. Therefore, rational agents will necessarily pursue their self-interest. In Foot's early view, various kinds of considerations, not only self-interest, give reasons that will move rational agents to act. Her middle period views are quite different—she gives up on the idea that there are descriptions that automatically give reasons, except in the case of self-interest. As she later states in *Natural Goodness*, she "rather inconsistently" held onto the idea that considerations of self-interest have independent reason-giving force (NG 10). Hence, she retains a remnant of her earlier Anscombian views. Again, the view is that considerations of self-interest necessarily move *rational* agents to action. Morality, by contrast, does not necessarily move rational agents; it moves morally good agents, and one can be rational without being morally good.

Her shift in view on reasons for action obviously did not entail a change from her early moral rationalism.[1] She could have continued to maintain that morality inevitably serves self-interest, and hence, that it necessarily gives us reasons. Yet, in renouncing both the idea that morality necessarily serves our self-interest as well as the idea that there are a variety of desirability characteristics that can give us reasons, the only option is to say that moral considerations depend on the contingent possession of relevant desires for their force. Foot never explicitly states the reasoning behind her middle period rejection of Anscombe's views. Possibly, the change went unnoticed by her in that she did not recognize the significant differences between Anscombe's views and the Humean account of reasons for actions she came to embrace. For Anscombe, when we understand someone to have a desire, we rely on evidence that they want something that can be construed as good, whereas in the Humean account, desires can be aimed at anything whatsoever. In Anscombe's account, desires play a significant but secondary role in rationalizing actions, with goods playing the primary role. Those goods are mentioned in the premises of practical syllogisms, which give support to practical conclusions that have validity, independent of our desires. Such syllogisms then move us to action in the presence of relevant desires. Since desires play an important role in Anscombe's account of action, there is some affinity with Hume's account.[2] Yet, despite some affinities, it is crucial to note how truly different these accounts are from each other. In what follows, I will elaborate and assess the position Foot arrived at in her middle period view of the rationality of morality.

Morality and etiquette

The term "hypothetical imperative" comes from Immanuel Kant's moral philosophy, in which it is contrasted with the "categorical imperative." A hypothetical imperative is a command, or ought-statement that depends for its reason-giving force on having a certain purpose. For example, someone's ability to say that I ought to purchase an airplane ticket to New York today depends on whether I have the purpose of going there. If I lack that purpose, or give up on it, then there is no sense in which one could continue to maintain that I ought to buy the ticket. By contrast, categorical imperatives do not depend on our possession of any special purpose for their reason-giving force; they have normative authority for us, regardless of our purposes. In "Morality as a System of Hypothetical Imperatives," Foot sets out to challenge the widely held assumption that morality must consist of categorical imperatives. She undertakes to show that the surface grammar of moral judgments, stating what we ought to do, morally speaking, is misleading; when we make claims about what someone ought to do, morally speaking, we certainly appear to be making categorical claims. We tell children that they should not fib even when a successful fib would serve the purpose of escaping blame or punishment. Yet, Foot argues that this appearance is deceptive, making her case for this point by means of drawing an analogy between morality and etiquette.

Etiquette and morality are unlike in many ways, but they both tell us what we ought to do. In fact, as Foot points out, rules of etiquette are usually presented in the same categorical form as moral considerations; etiquette tells us what must and must not be done, period. Imperatives like, "You should not discuss money," or "Don't make personal remarks" use a categorical form. Foot calls these "non-hypothetical uses" of ought (VV 160). Yet, Foot takes it to be obvious that one can rationally ignore the rules of etiquette. Hence, the rules of etiquette do not give me a reason unless I have the purpose of doing what I ought to do from the point of view of etiquette. Of course, there is still a sense in which the rules of etiquette are unconditional. I am "gauche" if I flaunt the requirements of etiquette, regardless of my purposes. Still, Foot thinks it cannot be said that I necessarily have reason to conform to those rules, drawing the conclusion that "if a hypothetical use of 'should' gave a hypothetical imperative, and a non-hypothetical use of 'should' gave a categorical imperative, then 'should' statements based on rules of etiquette, or rules of a club would be categorical imperatives" (VV 160–1). Yet, these "should" statements do not give us categorical imperatives. We therefore cannot trust the surface grammar of our "should" or "ought" statements to tell us whether we have a categorical or a hypothetical imperative.

Foot sees the commands of morality as similar to those of etiquette. Though they are stated in categorical form, there is no reason to think that someone who acts against them is necessarily irrational. It is perfectly plausible to think that they give reasons only if we have the purpose of doing what we should do from the moral point of view. As with etiquette, the claims of morality are, in some sense, unconditional—one does not escape being wicked simply by lacking the purpose of being moral. As Foot states, "the man who rejects morality because he sees no reason to obey its rules can be convicted of villainy but not of inconsistency" (VV 161). That is because such an amoral agent does not act against any purpose that he has, and is therefore not irrational.

The next question that Foot sets out to address is—what would be the implications for morality if it turns out that rules of morality are hypothetical imperatives? Many think that this would be a catastrophic situation. Kant, for example, thought that if morality were merely hypothetically imperative, we would only be moral when it served selfish and pleasure-seeking purposes. Yet, Foot argues that Kant had an inadequate view of human psychology, stating, "Quite apart from thoughts of duty a man may care about the suffering of others, having a sense of identification with them and wanting to help if he can" (VV 165). Of course, helping others with the purpose of promoting one's reputation for charity is not compatible with the virtue of charity, but one can simply desire to help others, and in that case, there is no need for a categorical imperative to prompt the charitable acts.

Justice, as Foot realizes, cannot be motivated by the same concern for the good of others. Justice notoriously comes into conflict with the good of others, as there may be cases where people would be well-served by a false accusation or the redistribution of money owed to a rich man to the poor. This leads Foot to posit that just persons are concerned with truth, liberty and that they "want every man to be treated with a certain respect" (VV 165). In Foot's view, then, a morally good agent has a variety of independent commitments that lend force to considerations of the well-being and the rights of others. She evidently thinks this is a plausible psychological picture that has not been given sufficient consideration, due to the assumption that morality consists of categorical imperatives.

At the conclusion of "Morality as a System of Hypothetical Imperatives," Foot makes an even bolder claim. She imagines that those resistant to her claim will think that we have a duty to adopt moral ends, yet she thinks that the idea that we have a duty to have certain ends is complete nonsense. It is, of course, trivially true that we ought *morally* to have moral ends; so that from the perspective of morally good people, these ends appear to be obligatory. However, the objection suggests a use of "ought" that is not tied to any particular institution, practice, or person's perspective, and she thinks it is merely an illusion that there is any such sense of "ought" (VV 167). In this respect, Foot claims she is offering a "defictionalized" vision of morality (VV 174). Before assessing her case against the categorical imperative in morality, I will look at a further elaboration of her case against fictions about morality from the same period.

Morality and Art

In "Morality and Art" (1970), Foot gives a fuller account of ways in which we tend to fictionalize our account of morality, arguing against moral rationalism by comparing moral judgment with aesthetic judgment. Whereas our views about morality are shrouded in fictions, our views on art are not. Foot says:

> Moral judgments regulate our conduct in just those areas which arouse the deepest feelings of guilt, so that we want to erect the strongest possible barriers against what we fear we might do; aesthetic judgments guide our conduct in relatively calm water when they guide it at all. (MD 15)

Despite the different ways these two sorts of judgment relate to our conduct, Foot thinks a comparison of our attitudes about them is illuminating. She isolates three ways in which we tend to distort our conception of moral judgments, whereas our parallel ideas about art seem to be more realistic. First, we overextend our claims to objectivity in moral judgment. She is not retracting her claim that there are moral facts, but rather qualifying the extent to which our morality is based on such facts. She argues that there are "definitional criteria" of moral good and evil, by which she means criteria that are attached to the concept of morality itself. Morality is necessarily aimed at "removing particular dangers and securing certain benefits" (MD 7). Based on such definitional criteria, it is clear that Hitler's treatment of the Jews was morally indefensible—a position that is consistent with Foot's early treatment of morality. Yet, to this early account, she now adds that outside of the definitional criteria, there is significant room for cultural variation and stipulation of moral norms. She writes, "It seems, for instance, that while one can determine from the concept of morality that there is an objection to murder one cannot determine completely what will count as murder" (MD 7). She thinks that we have a realm of choice in this matter. For example, she believes that it is a matter of stipulation whether to count a fetus as a person possessing the right to protection from killing. The decision whether or not to do so is what constitutes what Foot calls a "contingent principle" (MD 8). Of course, we do have strong feelings about these matters and use objective language to describe our judgments. Foot thinks it is not wrong to feel strongly about these matters, as we may be strongly committed to our judgments of taste, which are more obviously subjective. Yet, it is mistaken to speak as though some objective authority stands behind our judgments about such matters. In the realm of aesthetic judgment, Foot thinks that we do not tend to have the pretense of a higher authority. In the face of disagreement about a work of art, we appeal to reactions to the work—our own or those of others (MD 10).

Second, we tend to discount the possibility of relativism in morality while embracing it in art; yet, there is evidently some degree of relativism about moral judgments. This follows closely from the first point since, if we have contingent principles in morality, different societies and individuals can obviously adopt different contingent principles. But whereas we are uncomfortable with moral relativism, we acknowledge and embrace relativism in judgments of taste.

Third, echoing the point spelled out in "Morality as a System of Hypothetical Imperatives," she argues that we do not tend to view art as generating rationally compulsory judgments about what we ought to do, whereas we do think this about morality. She writes, "We would recognize it as nonsense to say 'The fact that a work of art is a good work of art is itself a reason for choosing it, and never mind whether you will get anything out of it or not' " (MD 19). And yet, people do say such things about morality when they hold that it generates categorical imperatives, which apply to individuals regardless of their purposes.

"Morality and Art" presents a view of morality with a limited claim to objectivity and no necessary reason-giving force. Foot seems remarkably calm about the implications of this view for our social life, stating:

> . . . some contingent principles would surely survive. People do care, for example, that individuals should not in everything be sacrificed for the good of others, or that the unborn should be counted as in the human community. They are ready to fight for such things; why should they not continue to do so? (MD 15)

The obvious rejoinder to this puzzling query is that if the moral principles which decide whether abortion is permissible are reduced to the level of our preference for Tolstoy over Dostoyevsky, or milk over rancid yak butter in our tea, then it is quite unclear how any disputes could be justified. It is also worth considering that the when we decide the boundaries of the definition of murder, there will be substantial consequences attached to such decisions. In most societies, whether someone has committed a serious crime deserving punishment will depend on our choice of contingent principles about the scope of murder. Could we possibly be justified in punishing someone based on a shared subjective commitment to the idea that a fetus is a person?

Further, Foot's comparison of moral and aesthetic judgment is flawed. She is correct to say that there is some appeal to our reactions to works of art in the discussion of aesthetic merit, but wrong to infer from this that judgments of aesthetic merit are merely subjective. We can assess sensitivity to aesthetic merits and recognize that some individuals have greater ability to appreciate works than we do ourselves; they have a response that the work merits.[3] Their praise for works may give us reason to attempt to understand works that are initially unmoving to us, and certainly we do not know with any finality that a work hitherto unmoving to us is therefore incapable of moving us. Hence, it may be that there is objectivity within at least some domains of aesthetic evaluation. The business of criticism is surely a matter of helping us to appreciate worthwhile works of art, and sometimes, it is indeed a matter of distinguishing good art from bad art.[4] Foot's discussion is also marred by a tendency to conflate areas of aesthetics that are arguably quite distinct, as fashion and standards of personal beauty may be quite distinct from the fine arts. We are ready to charge someone incapable of appreciating what we would call a masterpiece of fine art with defective taste, and we attempt to cultivate an appreciation for these works in young people, thinking that their lives will be enriched by enjoyment of these works. I conclude from these considerations that it is not obviously fictional to think of objective authority in aesthetic matters. Also, it is not complete nonsense to say that someone has reason to choose a good work of art, regardless of whether they will get anything out of it. After all, exposure to good works of art is the best way to come to appreciate them, and it is virtually impossible to know in advance whether one will appreciate a good work or not. The case of someone who is utterly incapable of appreciating what is universally acknowledged as a masterpiece, despite all efforts at education, seems more akin to a sociopath who is incapable of seeing any reason to take the suffering of others into account. In such a case, we may indeed say that the individual has no reason to look at works of art or, in the parallel case, to act morally, but the conclusions to draw from such cases are not as radical those Foot draws. It does not mean that the rest of us have no reason to pursue the presently lacking capacity for appreciation of good works of art or the presently lacking sensitivity to moral reasons, and so, Foot's argument does less than she takes it to have done to weaken the case for robust, objective moral authority and moral rationalism.[5]

The etiquette analogy examined

One disappointing feature of Foot's middle period case against moral rationalism is that it does not directly address her earlier arguments. As noted above, she simply states that morality does not always advance our self-interest because in individual cases, we are called on by morality to forgo great benefits or to make a heavy sacrifice. Yet, in her early writings, Foot acknowledged that morality does not advance our self-interest in that way.[6] Instead, she held then that the virtues are dispositions that generally advance our interests, and need not do so in every case; in adopting them, we are committing ourselves to a policy of choice which, on the whole, advances our interests. Still, one might think that the burden of proof must be on the advocate of morality as a system of categorical imperatives to show that morality cannot be plausibly conceived as a system of hypothetical imperatives. Foot seems to have shifted the burden of proof with her middle period piece, and, because she lost confidence in her earlier position, she did not take up the challenge of meeting that burden.

Yet, others have taken up that challenge. Michael Smith defends moral rationalism against Foot's middle period arguments, arguing that normative reason claims cannot all be hypothetical imperatives.[7] This is because we often think that those suffering from depression have reasons to do various things, for which they have no desire or interest. He therefore thinks that normative reason claims are better seen as ancillary to hypothetical desires; that is, normative reason claims are ancillary to the desires that we would have if we were fully rational, which, he argues, are nonrelative. All fully rational agents would have the same desires in the same circumstances. He concludes that normative reason claims are categorical imperatives because they tell us what we ought to do, regardless of our actual desires.

Foot has some reply to this argument. Contrary to Smith's claim, middle period Foot does not believe that all normative reason judgments are ancillary to our actual desires. Rather, she thinks that reasons of self-interest generate categorical imperatives. We might account for many of our intuitions concerning reasons that depressives have through reasons of self-interest. So, Smith's appeal to depressives does not necessarily carry as much weight against Foot as he thinks. Since she is not a consistent externalist, she does not, after all, think that all normative reason statements generate only hypothetical imperatives.

Smith also thinks that Foot's view leads to a mistaken idea of what motivates the morally good agent.[8] In Foot's view, a morally good agent must be committed to "doing what is morally right," where this is read *de dicto* rather than *de re*. This means that Foot's morally good agent aims at doing whatever falls under the heading of "morally right." By contrast, as we generally think of the morally good agent, she is motivated by a nonderivative concern for such things as practicing honesty, doing good for her friends and children, and getting people what they deserve. According to Smith, externalists such as Foot present the morally good person as having a single nonderivative moral concern with what is "morally right," and this concern is what Smith describes as a fetish or moral vice.

This raises two questions. First, why, in Smith's view, is Foot necessarily committed to such a conception of moral motivation? Second, if she is committed to such a conception, is it as troubling as Smith claims? On the first question, Smith's account certainly contradicts Foot's explicit position; after all, she claims that the morally good agent has a diverse set of aims, including concern for the well-being of others, honesty, and respect for an individual's rights. This sounds like the account which Smith thinks we ought to have regarding the motives of the morally good agent. Yet, the issue is whether Foot is entitled to that account of motivation, given her views about the nature of morality, and Smith thinks that she is not entitled to that account because morality, in her view, is an institution. The existence of morality depends on people taking each other's views on conduct seriously in regard to moral matters (VV 204). Of course, the standards of assessment must be related to human well-being in some relevant way for it to be a genuine morality, but there is also room, apparently, for individual societies to stipulate moral norms. Smith argues that with such an institutional view of morality, motivation to be moral would be much like motivation to follow the rules of etiquette.[9] Our motivation to follow the rules of etiquette is surely externally related to those rules. The existence of the system of etiquette depends on people taking up such a system as authoritative for their conduct, and their motivation for doing so is surely external to the system itself. They have reason to do what etiquette requires because they desire to do the "done thing," where that is read *de dicto* and not *de re*. That is to say, they use the proper fork, not for its own sake, but because it happens to fall under the label "the done thing" in our society. And that is a sensible thing to say about the motivations of a well-mannered individual; he respects the conventions of the society in which he finds himself, and these may very well change over time or from one society to the next. Yet, as we have seen, Smith thinks an account of moral motivation according to which we are motivated to do whatever falls under the label "morally right," is implausible. Instead, in moral matters, we expect people to be concerned with the right thing to do, where this is read *de re*.

Assuming, for the moment, that this is a proper account of the view to which middle period Foot is entitled, given her account of morality, let us move on to the question of whether the account is as objectionable as Smith believes. Arguably it is not. Sigrún Svavarsdóttir has argued that Smith is wrong to think that there is any moral vice attached to acting on the basis of what is morally right, where this is read *de dicto*.[10] Smith thinks that an externalist account of moral motivation such as we see in middle period Foot results in making a fetish of being moral, but Svavarsdóttir questions whether this is actually the case. Making a fetish of morality would mean transforming it into an obsession and being rigidly resistant to any questioning of its grounds, but there does not seem to be anything about Foot's externalist account that commits her to such fetishism. As Svavarsdóttir states, "A concern for being moral should not be confused with a rigorous obsession with morality or a resistance to examine hard reflective questions about morality."[11] Further, Svavarsdóttir points out that having such a concern for morality does not prevent a morally good person, as the externalist conceives her, from being fully committed to the ends that she sees as falling under the label "morally right" or "morally required." If the externalist must hold that a morally good person must constantly remind herself that her aims fell under the label "morally right" in order to maintain her commitment to them, there would certainly be a problem. But nothing commits the externalist to such an account. Rather, once the externalist's morally good person recognizes that a certain end falls under the label "morally right" and acquires the motivation to do it because of that fact, she would normally go on to acquire an independent motivation to pursue that end.[12] This means that Foot's idea that the morally good agent is committed to various ends can stand with the notion that the externalist's morally good person must have a desire to do what is morally right, read *de dicto*. Hence, Smith cannot be correct in his reading of middle period Foot's views on moral motivation after all; Smith does not successfully make his case that externalists, such as Foot, are committed to a troubling view of moral motivation.

Russ Shafer-Landau also defends moral rationalism by challenging Foot's analogy between morality and etiquette.[13] There is, he thinks, a relevant difference between morality and etiquette, which is that etiquette is conventional in origin whereas morality is not. Shafer-Landau writes, "Requirements of law, etiquette, etc. are only contingently applicable, and so only contingently reason-giving. Moral requirements do not exhibit this sort of contingency."[14] According to him, this gives us a reason to resist Foot's analogy between morality and etiquette. Although etiquette and morality both make demands that are, in one sense, categorical—they apply to us regardless of our desires and purposes—they are different in that the demands of morality are pervasive or inescapable in a different sense. The demands of morality are objective and apply across boundaries of culture and history, which is obviously not the case with the rules of etiquette. To assume that morality is conventional would beg the question against moral realism. So, if Foot cannot assume that morality is conventional, the analogical argument does not go through.

Of course, Foot did *not* assume that morality is conventional, but instead agrees that there is at least an objective core to anything that we can accurately describe as a moral code or a system of moral rules. That raises the question of whether she overlooked the disanalogy between them, which Shafer-Landau points out. The answer, I believe, is that she did not, because the alleged disanalogy is based on a misrepresentation of etiquette and law. There are definitional criteria pertinent to etiquette and law, just as with morality. That is, there are certain conditions that must be fulfilled in order to truly assert of a society that it has a system of law or etiquette. Of course, the definitional criteria for morality are substantial in that they specify what the rules must be *about* in order to be moral rules, but surely, there is also some stipulation of content involved in the definitional criteria of etiquette. If a code of conduct dips into rather serious matters, outside of matters concerning social decorum, it will be a code that is part of religion or morality, rather than of etiquette. For example, if a certain society requires one to bring an animal to sacrifice before a priest annually, this is clearly more than a requirement of etiquette. Of course, there is still much room for the conventional specification of etiquette and morality in Foot's view, but this does not necessarily beg the question against moral realism because there may still be some actions that are morally required and claims pertaining to those actions that are straightforwardly true. It might seem that the same cannot be said for something such as law or etiquette, but on a certain level of generality, this may not be true. It is always vulgar or gauche to ignore what is stipulated as the "thing to be done" in a system of etiquette, as it is always criminal to violate the law. This captures the sense in which the rules of each are pervasive, despite variations in content from one society to the next. I believe Shafer-Landau is wrong, then, in his claim to have located a disanalogy between morality and etiquette that undermines Foot's argument.

The case for the categorical imperative

We have seen that attempts to defuse Foot's argument by pointing out disanalogies between morality and etiquette are unpersuasive. Yet, there is a more direct approach to arguing against Foot, which is to show that hypothetical imperatives ultimately depend on categorical imperatives. As noted above, Foot admits that there are categorical imperatives inasmuch we are rationally required to be prudent, regardless of our actual purposes. But for Foot, these categorical imperatives are not behind the reason-giving force of hypothetical imperatives, such as those which she holds give force to moral reasons. Yet, according to Christine Korsgaard, hypothetical imperatives must be grounded in some sort of categorical imperative if they are to have any reason-giving force.

Korsgaard proposes two readings of the hypothetical imperative.[15] In the first, hypothetical imperatives tell us that we have reason to take means to ends, so long as there are reasons to pursue those ends. In that reading, the hypothetical imperative derives a reason from a reason. In the second reading, hypothetical imperatives tell us that we have reason to take means to ends that we have. The second reading derives a reason from a fact, and so derives an "ought" from an "is." If hypothetical imperatives are read in the first way, it is rather obvious that they do not ultimately tell us about what we have reason to do, and so, they must all depend on some other unconditional source of reasons. In the second reading, hypothetical imperatives could generate reasons without depending on an unconditional source, but, Korsgaard argues, it is not possible to derive reasons from facts about what we desire.

In the second reading, we do not have reason to pursue our ends, as we are simply going to pursue those ends. In this interpretation, the hypothetical imperative tells us what we have reason to pursue based on a prediction of what we will do. Yet, this understanding of hypothetical imperatives renders it impossible to violate them. Korsgaard discusses a commonplace example of practical irrationality—we set out to ride a roller coaster and then chicken out at the last minute. Viewed from the perspective of the second reading of the hypothetical imperative, this means that we were not going to ride the roller coaster after all, and so, had no reason to take the means to do so, and therefore there was no weakness of will or irrationality involved when we ceased to take the means to realize the supposed end; it really was not our end after all. In this reading of the hypothetical imperative then, it is meaningless to speak of being guided by reason or to think of ourselves as falling under any requirements. In the end, this view denies that there is any such thing as practical reason.

Clearly, this is not a conclusion that Foot seems prepared to accept, as she holds that those with a desire to be moral have reason to be moral, and she appears to think of this as a genuine requirement of rationality. Yet, this is not an argument in which her admission of a categorical imperative to be prudent helps. The categorical imperative commanding us to promote our self-interest is unconnected to whatever hypothetical imperatives we may have, thanks to our desires. Foot's account is what Korsgaard would call a "patchwork account" inasmuch as it integrates rationalism about reasons of self-interest.[16] Although the patchwork nature of Foot's account allows her to escape some criticism that comes to consistent externalists, Korsgaard argues that it is ultimately unsatisfactory as an overall account of practical reason. It takes for granted the reason-giving force of the reasons of self-interest; these considerations are dogmatically asserted to be reason-giving, while anything that is outside this range falls to the argument that Korsgaard makes against the hypothetical imperative in the second reading.

Is Foot incorrect in thinking that there can be self-standing hypothetical imperatives? As we will see in detail in Chapter 6, Foot in her later work rejects the idea of self-standing hypothetical imperatives and provides a nondogmatic account of reasons for action that is grounded in human nature. Later Foot agrees with Smith and Korsgaard that there must be some categorical imperatives, and she finds the source of those imperatives in claims about what is necessary in order to have a good human will.

Nothing yet said provides a definitive refutation of normative skepticism, of course. It only argues that practical reason depends on the existence of categorical imperatives, without proving that there are any. There is reason to agree that rejecting the idea that we have reasons to have certain desires means abdicating the idea of practical reason altogether. Derek Parfit argues that subjectivism about reasons leads to absurd consequences, such as not having reason to avoid a future filled with intense agony.[17] Yet, clearly, we have reason not to want that. It is only by dogmatically asserting the reason-giving force of considerations of self-interest that middle period Foot can dodge that bullet. A non-dogmatic rationalism clearly has its attractions, and I will argue in Chapter 6 that later Foot has a defensible account of that sort.

CHAPTER FOUR

Virtue and morality

"The study of ethics had been, for philosophers such as Aristotle and Aquinas, largely a study of the virtues, and as the foundations of Western morality had been laid down by Greek and Christian thinkers it would be surprising if we could neglect this topic without loss." (MD 105)

Foot and Anscombe on virtue

As shown in Chapter 2, virtues play a prominent role in Foot's moral philosophy beginning with her earliest articles.[1] "Virtues and Vices" (1977) gives a comprehensive discussion regarding the nature of virtues and their relation to the goodness of persons and their actions. Yet, it gives a spare account of her motivations for examining virtue, and further, it is not clear whether it is appropriate to regard Foot as a virtue ethicist in the current sense of the term. In this chapter, I will examine Foot's treatment of virtues and their relation to morality, which will help put us in a better position to examine her nonconsequentialist treatment of moral problems in the next chapter. I will begin by addressing the question—why, according to Foot, are the virtues important for moral philosophy? I will then give an account of what constitutes a virtue in Foot's view, and discuss some developments in her approach to justifying the virtues. Finally, I will turn to questions about the relation of virtue to morality in Foot's account. The treatment I give here will take into account Foot's writing prior to her late works such as

Natural Goodness. This late piece gives us a different account of the virtues and will be discussed in Chapter 6.

According to Foot, it was reflection on the virtues that made her question the sharp division between fact and value embraced by emotivists and prescriptivists. She states, "It was reading Aquinas on the individual virtues that first made me suspicious of contemporary theories about the relation between 'fact' and 'value'" (VV xiii). As noted in Chapter 1, both Stevenson and Hare acknowledge that virtues appear to bridge fact and value. They admit that some facts simply amount to an action being courageous, yet they do not believe that we are in any way required to use virtue terms, and so, these terms fall to a subsidiary place in noncognitivist moral philosophy. In their view, virtue terms would only be used by someone who endorses a more fundamental set of norms for good behavior that would make the purportedly virtuous dispositions praiseworthy. Both Foot and Anscombe reject this argument. For them, the virtues are essential to morality, and as such, they should be the focus of our moral philosophy. Indeed, Anscombe goes so far as to call for a halt to work in moral philosophy in order to work on philosophy of psychology. She argues that the concept of a virtue must be treated before we can make progress in moral philosophy. As Anscombe writes:

> In present-day philosophy an explanation is required how an unjust man is a bad man, or an unjust action a bad one; to give such an explanation belongs to ethics; but it cannot even be begun until we are equipped with a sound philosophy of psychology. For the proof that an unjust man is a bad man would require a positive account of justice as a 'virtue'. This part of the subject-matter of ethics is, however, completely closed to us until we have an account of what *type of characteristic* a virtue is – a problem, not of ethics, but of conceptual analysis – and how it relates to the actions in which it is instanced; a matter which I think Aristotle did not succeed in really making clear.[2]

Foot endorses this program, and indeed, I believe this statement by Anscombe precisely captures the motives behind Foot's work on the virtues. Foot's aim, then, is to vindicate the fundamental significance of the virtues for a proper understanding of the place of value in nature. This concern can be situated within the metaphysics of value, which both Anscombe and Foot approach through conceptual analysis. As we have seen in Chapter 2, Foot argues that to have a moral view, such as the view that stealing is wrong, it is necessary not only to endorse a general rule of behavior, but also to have a broader set of cognitive and emotional responses to the behavior in question. These responses register the impact of the behavior in view of a conception of what is good for human beings. In the absence of such responses, one may have principles of behavior, but we would have no reason to call them *moral* principles as they lack the appropriate connection to concern for human well-being. Foot's concern with the virtues comes from this fundamental question about the nature of morality and its place within nature, not from normative disagreements with existing frameworks or concerns about a misguided moral psychology. As we will see, Foot rejects consequentialism, the view that we are morally required to bring about the best overall state of affairs, and she does not embrace a Kantian conception of rationality; yet, her rejection of these positions stems from her views on the nature of value and her findings about the virtues rather than the other way around.

Virtue as a disposition of the will

As Anscombe argued, there is an issue of philosophical psychology that must be settled in order to discern whether virtue indeed deserves a fundamental role in our theory of value. We need to know what type of characteristic a virtue is in order to know whether being just is a virtue, whether possession of it makes one good, and, if it does make one good, how it does so. In Foot's account, there are three essential features of a virtue—first, a virtue is a disposition of the will; second, it is beneficial either to others, or to its possessor as well as to others; third, it is corrective of some bad general human tendency.

Let us start with the idea that a virtue is a disposition of the will. Clearly, there are dispositions throughout nature that do not involve the will, such as the fragility of glass. When Foot uses the term "disposition," however, she appears to have in mind a concept that originates with Aristotle and is developed by Aquinas, and this concept is narrower in scope than the general concept of a disposition that covers such features of nature. Aristotle defined virtue as a kind of *hexis* (ἕξις), a term which Aquinas translates into Latin as *habitus*, and both of these terms are, in turn, usually translated into English as "disposition." Unlike our term "disposition," the original terms refer to characteristics of individuals with minds, and so such dispositions are not found in inanimate objects. And while Aquinas's term, *habitus* looks familiar to us in its resemblance to our term "habit," it would be misleading to use that term as a translation for *habitus*. As Anthony Kenny points out, as Aquinas defines *habitus*, it includes health, beauty, virtues, and vices, as well as various forms of knowledge and practical competencies.[3] Whereas there are habits that promote health and beauty, those qualities themselves are obviously not habits. For Aquinas, who here follows Aristotle directly, a *habitus* is a state that "is either a good state or a bad state for its possessor either absolutely or relatively."[4] These states are principles of action, Aquinas tells us, and the good state enables us to act in accordance with our nature. Health, unfortunately, is a state that is responsive to our wills only in some respects, and for Aquinas, responsiveness to the will is an important characteristic of all *habitus*. Indeed, this is the feature of *habitus* that distinguishes them from habits. As Kenny helpfully points out, possessing a habit usually makes it harder not to do something, whereas possessing a *habitus* makes it easier to do something. Smoking is a habit, if not an addiction, whereas generosity or speaking French is a *habitus*.[5] It is somewhat puzzling, then, that Aquinas considers health to be a *habitus*. Nevertheless, he believes there is a sense of health that involves the will; the soul can, in his view, act on the body in such a way as to promote its responsiveness to the will, as occurs when we do such things as exercise and eat well, and this is the sense of health in which it is properly considered a *habitus*.[6] As Foot's view treats the virtues as dispositions in this sense, I will henceforth use the term "disposition" to translate Aquinas's term, *habitus*.

Since all such dispositions involve the will, it may seem redundant to define the virtues as "dispositions of the will." Yet, the will itself, in this view, can be more or less responsive to reason. What does it mean for the will to be responsive to reason? What, after all, is the will? As we will see, to say that the virtues are "dispositions of the will," as Foot does, masks diversity among the virtues; and yet, despite this diversity, the will plays an important role in all of the virtues.

Foot starts her investigation of the connection between the virtues and the will by examining the role of intentions in determining someone's character. We evaluate someone's moral quality, she thinks, primarily by examining his intentions (VV 4). Yet, good intentions are not sufficient to demonstrate that someone is virtuous; in the case of charity or benevolence, one can show lack of charity if, despite one's good intentions, one fails to bring about the intended good. For example, one can be ignorant of something one should have known, as famously illustrated by Foot with her example of one failing to learn basic first aid. Someone who is genuinely benevolent will take the trouble to find out about basic first aid, and because such knowledge is so easily attained and so generally useful to others, it shows a lack of charity to fail to attain such knowledge. Also, Foot points out that our failures of performance can count against our virtue despite our good intentions when our heart is not in the action. Virtues are therefore also "dispositions of the heart," according to Foot, meaning that we must take the trouble to cultivate the desire to act well. Conversely, virtue *par excellence* occurs in one who is "prompt and resourceful" in doing good (Ibid.). A virtuous agent will take pleasure in doing good things for others, and so, for Foot, the will includes our intentions as well as our "innermost desires."

There are plenty of qualifications to add here. Surely, it is not always in our power to effect changes in our emotions and desires; at least, whether it is possible is an open question and subject to psychological inquiry.[7] Still, Foot has made a conceptual claim that is important here—we are charitable when our intentions and desires, *to the extent that these are under the control of our will*, are such that we can act for the good of others with ease and pleasure. If, due to a psychological condition such as depression, we cannot take joy in helping others, then this does not count against our possession of virtue. In fact, Foot thinks that such cases increase "the virtue that is needed if a man is to act well" (VV 14). But we must tread carefully here, for she does not mean that one in such a circumstance is necessarily more virtuous than one who is not. Yet, facing a condition such as depression may test our virtue; its onset may lead one to fail to act in accordance with virtue, while an equally virtuous nondepressed agent could carry on. To speak more generally, some people will find themselves in circumstances— psychological or social—that will make greater demands on their commitment to goodness.[8] This means that those who have a relatively easy time acting courageously or benevolently simply have not had their commitment to goodness tested in the same way as someone who faces psychological obstacles. Those who face such obstacles must *show* more virtue, though they are not necessarily more virtuous than those in more ideal circumstances.

The virtue of wisdom presents another set of problems for the connection of virtue with the will, which is essential to Foot's account. Unlike other virtues, wisdom seems primarily to be an excellence of the intellect rather than the will. Yet, just because a putative virtue concerns the intellect does not mean that the will is not also essential to it, as Foot argues. For her, wisdom has two components. First, it includes knowledge of the all-purpose means to very general good ends. She includes here ends such as "friendship, marriage, the bringing up of children, or the choice of ways of life" (VV 5). Such knowledge is within the reach of anyone who wants it since one need not be especially clever in order to acquire it and, in this way, it is unlike specialized scientific knowledge, which is something within the grasp of a lucky few who possess the necessary talent and opportunity to pursue it. This means that the knowledge involved in wisdom is within the scope of the will—we can get it if we want it, and therefore, we can be fairly evaluated for our success or failure in its realization.

The second part of wisdom, according to Foot, consists of knowing the worth of particular ends, something which she claims is difficult to describe. Here, she has in mind the knowledge involved in realizing that a life spent in the pursuit of wealth or fame at the expense of good relationships is, in fact, a wasted life. This aspect of virtue is a matter of forming judgments about what is worthwhile in life, and she thinks one can make false judgments about these matters. One wonders here how having a false view of what is worthwhile in life can be a matter that is under the control of one's will. Yet, Foot believes that there is a connection with the will here as well, stating, "Wisdom in this second part is . . . to be described in terms of apprehension, and even judgement, but since it has to do with a man's attachments it also characterises his will" (VV 7).

Yet, surely, this connection with the will is importantly different from the connection with the will in the case of other virtues, including the first aspect of wisdom. It seems important not only that the virtues characterize the will, but also that they are responsive to the will. Only if the virtues are responsive to the will can one impute a defect to someone who lacks a virtue because they could have acquired it, had they made the appropriate choices. The second aspect of wisdom does not seem to answer to the will in this way. Surely people of intelligence and integrity have arrived at questionable judgments about what is worthwhile in life, perhaps in large part through residing in a culture that reinforces faulty judgments, say, about women or other races. It may be sufficient to count as wise, in a sense that is subject to moral evaluation, that one competently *aspires* to true judgments about what is worthwhile in life. We may, compatibly with this view, take there to be another sense of wisdom that designates the successful attainment of a true conception of what is worthwhile in life, but wisdom in this sense seems to be a matter of good fortune. Wisdom would then have a properly moral sense that is different from the intellectual sense, and in this sense of wisdom is a disposition of the will.

The goodness of virtue

As described in Chapter 2, Foot in her early work embraces the view that the virtues necessarily benefit their possessors. She abandons that view in her middle period in favor of one in which the virtues are beneficial "in some general way" (VV 2). The benefit of the virtues may go to both their possessors and to others, or else, exclusively to others. Courage, temperance, and wisdom fall in the first category—benefiting both their possessors and others. She believes that charity and justice sometimes fall in the second category because they sometimes require their possessors to sacrifice everything (VV 3). Yet, as in "Morality as a System of Hypothetical Imperatives," Foot again fails to address her earlier arguments that this is no objection to the idea that the virtues are necessarily beneficial, in the sense that it is in their nature to benefit their possessors (VV 129). Justice, as she notes, poses the biggest problem for the idea that virtues necessarily benefit their possessors (VV xv, 2). Yet, it is also unclear that justice necessarily benefits others, at least on any given occasion; surely, there are cases in which we could benefit someone by means that infringe her rights, just as there are clearly occasions in which we can do great benefit for many others, but only by violating another's rights. So, there are, no doubt, occasions on which the demands of justice require that we renounce certain benefits that we could otherwise provide to others. But Foot seems to think that overall, it is beneficial for a society to consist of just individuals. As she states, "communities where justice and charity are lacking are apt to be wretched places to live, as Russia was under the Stalinists, or Sicily under the Mafia" (VV 3). In this qualified sense, then, the virtues are good in that they are beneficial.

Foot raises the question of whether virtue always results in good action and, in "Virtues and Vices," she affirms that it does. One difficulty is to account for the appearance that someone who is engaging in a bad action may still exhibit a virtue. She gives the example of a fearless murderer—does the fearless murderer exhibit courage? Foot thinks that the appearance that he does is misleading. She allows that we may be inclined to say that an act "took courage" or to speak of the "courage of the murderer," but we still resist calling it a "courageous act" or an "act of courage." In "Von Wright on Virtue" (1989), Foot adds that we may be willing to describe an action as an "act of courage" in cases where "the evil end is distant from the action concerned, as when, for instance, a man does something to save his own life or that of his companions in the course of some wicked enterprise, such as an unjust war" (MD 114). She believes this implies that courage is more than a simple mastery of fear; instead, it is mastery of fear in the context of the pursuit of good ends. Therefore, courage overlaps with daring and boldness, but since these conditions may exist in the absence of any commitment to goodness, they are not identical with the virtue of courage. We may say, instead, that the mastery of fear is a necessary, but not a sufficient, condition for the possession of courage.

Foot's arguments attempt to show that the virtues are beneficial qualities that produce good actions. One might think that this should be enough to establish that the virtues make one a good human being, but one more step is needed as it is not yet clear whether the virtues are necessary for one to be a good human being. Foot argues that the virtues are needed for humans as a corrective to general human characteristics that make it difficult for us to act well. In the case of virtues such as courage and temperance, it is rather obvious that we are susceptible to feeling fear in ways that make it difficult for us to achieve worthwhile goals, and that similar difficulties are posed by the temptations of pleasure. In the cases of charity and justice, there are deficiencies of motivation due to the fact that we are generally not as attached to the well-being and rights of others as we are to our own (VV 9). These tendencies are general, and need not be exhibited in individual cases (VV 10). As I noted above, some individuals might find it relatively easy to exhibit certain virtues, yet this is just an aspect of the circumstances of their lives, and it counts neither for nor against their possession of virtue, and it does not matter for the purpose of determining whether the virtues make one good *qua* human.

Since no disposition of the will can count as a virtue unless it is a corrective, according to Foot's view in her middle period, "everything is seen to depend on what human nature is like" (VV 10). She clearly believes that the traditional cardinal virtues (courage, temperance, justice, charity, and wisdom) deserve a place among the virtues as she construes them. Still she admits:

> It is possible . . . that the traditional list of the virtues and vices puts too much emphasis on hedonistic and sensual impulses and does not sufficiently take account of less straightforward inclinations such as the desire to be put upon and dissatisfied, or the unwillingness to accept good things as they come along. (Ibid.)

In Foot's view, then, our theory of human nature must be taken into account in our moral theorizing, and we must acknowledge as well that our theory of human nature is open to revision.

Foot's argument about the virtues is complex, but can be presented as follows:

1 A virtue is a disposition of the will that is needed by human beings, that is generally beneficial, and that makes its possessor's actions good.

2 Justice, charity, wisdom, courage, and temperance are dispositions of the will that are needed by human beings, are generally beneficial, and make their possessor's actions good.

3 So, justice, charity, wisdom, courage, and temperance are virtues.

4   Anything that is needed by human beings that is generally beneficial and that makes their actions good, in turn, makes human beings good, and the absence of it makes them bad.

5   Therefore, justice, charity, wisdom, courage, and temperance make someone good as a human being, and the absence of any of these makes one bad.

In Foot's view, the goodness that is realized in possessing the virtues extends beyond moral goodness; for example, she argues that one may show courage in confronting something fearsome for the sake of one's own life (MD 115). The idea here, which she develops in her later work, is that one does not act well in neglecting one's own interests, just as one who neglects the rights or well-being of others is defective. Human goodness encompasses more than moral goodness, and virtues are connected with human goodness thus broadly understood.

An objection to Foot's account of virtue

In one of the most carefully constructed critical treatments of Foot's work on the virtues, William Prior argues that Foot's account founders because she lacks a complete account of *eudaemonia*, a Greek term central to Aristotle's theory of virtue that is usually translated as "flourishing" or "happiness."[9] A good human being is a flourishing human being. If it is true that Foot lacks a complete account of flourishing, this would mean that she has an undeveloped notion of intrinsic goodness because she does not address the notion of human goodness at the center of her account. In other words, Prior questions whether Foot has sufficient grounds to assert premise (4) above. Further, he claims that to detach virtue from a detailed conception of *eudaemonia* results in an account of virtue that is "vague and incomplete."[10] Prior believes that Foot's account compares unfavorably with Aristotle's because he possessed a very well developed account of the human good. In Aristotle's account, according to Prior, "The good of the agent is the full development of our natural powers, and of our highest power, which is reason."[11] Reason is key to Aristotle's account of the human good, in Prior's reading, because in this account, "every act that makes excellent use of reason, every virtuous act, contributes essentially to the good life of an agent."[12]

Aristotle's view, at least in Prior's reading, yields a much tighter connection between virtue and the good of the agent than Foot claims for virtue in her account. According to Prior's reading of Aristotle, virtuous actions are *always* beneficial to the agent because they are intrinsically good, and this turns out to be the case "whatever the circumstances of the action might be, and whatever the consequential harms of the action might be."[13] As Prior realizes, this claim seems strongly counterintuitive since it requires us to believe that someone who must sacrifice his life or endure great pain in the course of virtuous action will still enjoy the intrinsic goodness of his action. To be precise, Prior states that "such actions are not cases of sacrificing everything but cases of preserving certain values without which life is not worth living."[14] Foot, by contrast, believes that there is a serious difficulty with virtues such as justice and charity because she does see laying down one's life in the course of a virtuous action as a total sacrifice. This may be behind her change of view on the benefits to be derived from acting virtuously from her position in "Moral Beliefs," in which she holds that virtues necessarily benefit their possessors, to her position in "Virtues and Vices," where she makes the much weaker claim that the virtues are beneficial in some general way. Prior thinks that Foot's vacillation on this issue is due to her refusal to squarely face the issue of *eudaemonia*.

Prior enumerates many other ways in which he believes Aristotle's account yields more determinate answers than Foot provides through his greater specificity about the human good. But the basic criticism should be clear. The question is clearly then—is Foot's account truly less specific than Aristotle's about the human good? Prior, I believe, exaggerates the difference between Aristotle and Foot on virtue; reason is clearly a central component of her conception of virtue in "Virtues and Vices" and, as we will see, it becomes even more central in her later work. She makes clear at the outset of "Virtues and Vices" that her major influences are Aristotle and Thomas Aquinas, and from them, she appears to take the idea that the virtues, as dispositions of the will, involve the application of reason. With apparent approval, she cites a passage from Aquinas on temperance, in which he says that the passions "may incite us to something against reason."[15] Further, wisdom would evidently not play such an important role in Foot's account of virtue if reason were not one of its essential features. Therefore,

Prior's objection must be that Foot does not clearly define the role of reason in constituting the flourishing that is achieved through acting in accordance with virtue, and hence, she does not clarify the role of reason in the human good.

The issue here appears more difficult than Prior acknowledges in his criticism of Foot. He seems to assume that if someone realizes an intrinsic good through his action, then his life is better for it, making it not only intrinsically good, but also *good for* the agent. Yet, this is not clearly true—presumably, a virtuous agent would appreciate the goodness of his action when he acts well, and on those occasions, acting well would contribute to his happiness. Yet, he clearly could produce goodness in action that is nevertheless inappreciable due to the circumstances in which it occurs. As Aristotle himself famously states, "Some maintain. . .that we are happy when we are broken on the wheel, or fall into terrible misfortunes, provided that we are good. Whether they mean to or not, these people are talking nonsense."[16] With this, Aristotle rejects the view, associated with Socrates, that no harm can befall a good man.[17] Foot rejects this view as well, most explicitly in *Natural Goodness*, where she states that happiness is the *enjoyment of good things* and such enjoyment is not identical with the goodness of virtue itself (NG 97). In the view that Foot opposes, any good that I could attain only by acting viciously will not count as a loss to a fully virtuous agent. The fully virtuous agent sees himself as having no reason to pursue freedom from the torture rack if doing so would mean being cowardly. In that view, the virtuous agent on the rack is acting well and therefore living well and flourishing. Foot resists the identification of living well with happiness. Though the virtuous agent in such a circumstance can live well, he cannot *enjoy* this activity, and so he is suffering and unhappy even as he acts well.

We can see that there are substantive issues separating Prior and Foot, but it is not due to Foot's lack of a well-developed account of *eudaemonia*. Instead, they appear to have distinct interpretations concerning the relationship of the goodness of virtue to a flourishing life. The question remains of who has the correct understanding of Aristotle, which goes well beyond the scope of this book. Yet, even if Prior does get Aristotle right, it is nevertheless unclear that he and Aristotle have the upper hand on the issues that would then divide them from Foot.

Virtue and morality

As shown in Chapter 2, the virtues are an essential component of morality, in Foot's view. We can attribute moral judgments only to those who have roughly virtuous responses to actions in light of their putative impact on human well-being; we need not agree on what is virtuous and vicious, but we must register our understanding of our actions' impact on human beings with gladness or sorrow when they bring help or harm. Despite this common feature to moral judgments, there is still significant room for moral differences. To use an example from Foot's "When is a Principle a Moral Principle?", a group of people might find it wrong to wear brightly colored clothing. Initially, it is perplexing how this could be a moral view. Yet, if it is discovered that they regard this behavior as ostentatious, and, say, distracting from a proper concern with healthy social relations and piety, then their judgment starts to become intelligible as a moral one, even if we question the premises they marshal to support it. For Foot, this indicates that morality goes beyond what can be captured by philosophical discussion of the virtues. There is room for individual societies to specify a "moral system" or "system of virtue" (MD 75, 103). Hence, in her view, there is no straightforward path from the virtues to a criterion of right action, and to suggest as much courts a fiction about the power of philosophical reflection.[18] Rather, members of human communities face a constructive, social task of devising a moral code, and evaluating these moral codes is a matter that is partly independent of the virtues. In fact, Foot appears to favor the contractualist views of John Rawls and Tim Scanlon as providing viable criteria for evaluating moral systems (MD 103–4). Rawls and Scanlon believe that we can evaluate proposed moral norms from the perspective of a hypothetical social contract.

All of this suggests that it may be incorrect to regard Foot as a virtue ethicist, at least in the contemporary sense of the term, as one of the main components of contemporary virtue ethics is to develop a criterion of right action based on the virtues.[19] For example, Hursthouse offers the following criterion—"An action is right iff it is what a virtuous agent would characteristically do in the circumstances."[20] Foot seems to explicitly distance herself from this project in her final publication "Rationality and Goodness" (2004). There, she states, "[P]hilosophers such as Rosalind Hursthouse,

Christine Swanton, and Michael Slote . . . insist that dispositions, motives and other 'internal' elements are the primary determinants of moral goodness and badness. I myself have never been a 'virtue ethicist' in this sense. For me it is *what is done* that stands in this position" (RG 2). Unfortunately, this statement is misleading and unclear in that it lumps together virtue ethicists who take quite different positions. Specifically, Hursthouse and Swanton do not take the view that internal elements are the primary determinants of moral goodness and badness, as Foot suggests. Doing wrong is one important aspect of acting badly, in their view, and clearly, the appeal to the virtuous agent does not require the individual to act from virtuous motives. For them, a virtuous agent is better than one who merely acts in accordance with virtue, and hence does what is right, but surely, Foot would agree with that. She seems to be much closer to Hursthouse's view than her statement would suggest.[21]

Setting aside the issue of whether her claims about others are accurate, let us turn to what that statement suggests about her own views. She appears to distance herself from the derivation of a criterion of right action from the virtues. There are at least two reasons she might wish to do this—the first being that, in her view, the virtues do not specify right action in the absence of a moral code or system, and this is something that is stipulated or constructed by societies with appeal to the virtues. Yet, some attempt to codify justice and charity, among other virtues, is only a necessary condition for a code to be a moral code, in her view. The evaluation of moral systems goes beyond the virtues, and she endorses two criteria for its assessment—first, a good moral system can demand reciprocity from anyone because of the good it does for him. Second, it has to be such that anyone could conform to it and live well "in the ordinary, nonmoral, sense" (MD 103–4). These criteria are inspired by Rawls' and Scanlon's moral contractualism, and they do not fall out of simple reflection on the virtues. Instead, they are the result of Foot's deep reflection on the nature of moral systems, as well as her arguments against the idea that the goal of morality is to produce the best state of affairs, arguments to which I return below.

A second possible reason for Foot to reject the attempt to derive a criterion of right action from the virtues is that she may think that such a criterion does not track the features of right actions that make them right and, conversely, makes wrong actions wrong. That is, what is wrong about an act of injustice is not that a virtuous agent would not do it, but that it is an act in which someone's rights are violated. Of course, a just agent takes violations of rights seriously and would not deliberately violate anyone's rights. The virtuous agent tracks those features that make such actions wrong, and these are a product of a specific moral code. We are bound to ask what happens when the moral code of one's society makes unfair demands; surely, under such circumstances, we are deeming the code unfair by postulating an idealized version of that moral code, purged of whatever makes it unfair.

Justice, charity, and morality

In "Morality, Action, and Outcome" (1985), Foot states, "No decision is more important for practical ethics than that by which we come to embrace or reject utilitarianism" (MD 88). Foot rejects utilitarianism for two reasons—first, she thinks that utilitarianism depends on a mistaken consequentialist theory of value. Second, she thinks that all who are guided by such a conception of value make mistakes about the nature of morality.

Foot believes that consequentialism depends on the notion that there is such a thing as a "good state of affairs" and she thinks that utilitarians and consequentialists are mistaken in thinking that there is such a thing. She endorses an argument made by Peter Geach, according to whom there is no such thing as the property of goodness *simpliciter*.[22] "Good," according to Geach, is an attributive adjective, and therefore has no sense when it is not coupled with a kind that fixes a relevant way in which something can be good. For example, "good event" does not have a sense, at least without taking into account the interests of the person who is uttering those words. Foot takes Geach's argument to raise the question of whether the phrase "good state of affairs" is like "good event" in lacking a sense when meant in the way that consequentialists must mean it (MD 63, 97).

Of course, people will speak of events as being "a good thing," as, for example, when a favored sports team achieves a victory or a number of people are unexpectedly rescued from a disaster. The first example is a case in which talk of a "good thing" or "good state of affairs" is speaker-relative (MD 64); that is, something is deemed "good" in view of the speaker's interests. In the second case, we may be tempted to say that what we mean is "good, from an impersonal point of view." Surely, in such a case, it is not merely good from my point of view that the people have been saved; when I have no personal stake in the outcome, it is clear that it is not in my interest that more people are saved. The idea, then, is that the state of affairs is good from the perspective of everyone—it is a state of affairs that is generally advantageous. Hence, such claims seem to lead us toward utilitarianism. Foot replies here, "an account of the idea of good states of affairs which simply defines it in terms of maximum welfare is no help to us here. For our problem is that something is supposed to be being said *about* maximum welfare and we cannot figure out what this is" (MD 67). That is to say, "maximum welfare" has a sense, but the utilitarian is trying to say that the "best state of affairs" is one in which maximum welfare is realized, and it is the sense of this latter phrase that is being queried by Foot.

An alternative view of what it means to say that it is a "good thing" when people are saved from disaster is that it is "good from a moral point of view." In one interpretation, the phrase "good from a moral point of view" means "good from my perspective as a benevolent person." So, in that interpretation, this is a case of the speaker-relative use of "good." But Foot notes that I, as a benevolent person, would not deem it a good thing if one person were deliberately killed in order to save five. Such a situation is commonly illustrated in an imaginary case called "Transplant," in which a talented surgeon has five patients, each needing different organs, and they can all be saved by a healthy patient who serendipitously walks into his office. Most people would find it wrong, indeed, very wrong, for the doctor to carve up the healthy patient to help the five. Benevolence is not the only relevant virtue here; justice, which bids us to respect an individual's rights, requires us not to take the life of the one, even for the sake of saving many. There is no sense that attaches to the idea of a "better state of affairs," according to which it is a "good thing" to carve up the one to save five. The idea of better states of affairs makes sense, Foot claims, from "within morality," as in this case, it expresses a benevolent agent's concern with saving the greatest number of people possible, but only when doing so is compatible with the virtues. The virtuous agent would not admit the possibility that an unjust act could produce a better state of affairs.

Foot believes that consequentialists take a concept that has a sense within morality and attempt to move it to a "criterial position outside it" (MD 75). Namely, consequentialists hold that the sole justification of a moral code is that it maximizes welfare and thereby produces the best state of affairs. This is a tempting thought as we tend to think of moral codes as a kind of tacit legislation, and utilitarianism is surely a sensible way to think of legislation—our laws, tacit or otherwise, should attempt to bring about the greatest good for all. Yet, Foot thinks that this is just a consequentialist assumption about the aim of morality. Who, she asks, is supposed to have this shared end of promoting the greatest good of all? In the case of actual laws, we could assign this to the role of the legislators, but it is not obvious that morality requires us to have a shared end, and if not, it may best be seen as a compromise between individuals pursuing their individual ends (MD 76).

According to Foot, our actual morality is a "mixed" aim-and-rule morality, not a system directed to a single aim (MD 101). Some rules of morality are not like "see to it that there is less shouting," but rather like "do not shout" (MD 99). Our common sense morality contains rules that formulate what are sometimes cast as "deontological restrictions" on acting for the greatest good. That is, they tell us that we have a duty to do something (not kill, not lie, keep our promises) that holds even when doing so would produce seemingly worse outcomes. Of course, Foot can reject the appearance by saying the apparent worse outcome comes from applying the notion of a "best state of affairs."

Yet, as Samuel Scheffler forcefully argues, there are problems with justifying such deontological moral rules, and these problems can be raised without appealing to the notion of the "best state of affairs."[23] Let us take a rule that forbids lying—such a rule tells us that lying is morally objectionable; as Foot would have us read it, it would be wrong to lie even when the lie would prevent more lies from being told. Scheffler asks us, "How . . . can it be rational to forbid the performance of a morally objectionable action that will have the effect of minimizing the total number of comparably objectionable actions that are performed and will have no other morally relevant consequences?"[24] In formulating this objection, Scheffler is not appealing to the idea that it is a worse state of affairs if more lies are told, only to the idea that the violations are morally objectionable, which seems to be implied by the rule itself. It appears that Foot could say that Scheffler's objection implies that we have a moral aim that we do not, in fact, have—namely, minimizing the occurrence of violations of the rule. Yet, Scheffler anticipates this response and argues that this view has unacceptable consequences. As he states:

> Defenders of such views are unlikely to claim that the relevant standard of assessment includes agent-centered restrictions, but that it is a matter of indifference, from the vantage point represented by that standard whether or not those restrictions are violated. For if it is not the case that it is preferable, from that vantage point, that no violations should occur than that any should, it is hard to see how individual agents could possibly be thought to have reason to observe the restrictions when doing so did not happen to coincide with their own interests or the interests of those they cared about.[25]

Here, Scheffler aims to box Foot into a dilemma. If the violation of rules is morally objectionable, this gives me a reason to try to prevent them, and that would make it paradoxical to suggest that I would not have a reason to do something immoral to prevent a great number of immoral acts. If the violation of rules is not morally objectionable, then it would seem that I only have reason to avoid violating them or to prevent others from doing so when it is in my interest to do so.

As Foot notes in a review of Scheffler's book, "Laws apply to persons in that they forbid them to do certain things: no one suggests that it cannot be illegal to do what will minimize the number of illegal acts."[26] Foot appears to have a point here; yet, it raises a question about the rationality of our legal system. After all, it would arguably be unjust to punish someone who kills another when the victim in question was demonstrably on a course to commit murder himself, all the more so if he were on track to commit multiple murders. This might not be something made explicit in our rules, but may instead be part of the accepted understanding of the laws and part of judicial practice. If the law does not explicitly permit the commission of illegal acts to prevent the commission of a greater number of illegal acts, this may have to do with an astute assessment of the negative consequences of vigilantism. That is, we may have reasons to deter untrained people from attempting to enforce the law on their own, and hence punish people who attempt to do so even when their individual acts are on balance for the good. Yet, in the moral case, we are considering whether that individual's act was good, and if we say that it was not, then we need to explain how we can have reason to avoid killing when it could be done for the sake of avoiding a greater number of killings. In other words, considerations of the general consequences of a legal system should undoubtedly enter our deliberation about what to deem illegal. Similar considerations would also enter in framing our moral code inasmuch as we offer each other explicit rules for the guidance of conduct. Yet, in framing a legal or moral code, we presumably make reference to a system of values that applies to outcomes and actions; when a legal or moral code insists on punishing or blaming a good action, which it clearly can, it owes us an account of why that should be done, and such an account can be provided in the case of vigilantism.

Foot does not succeed in defusing Scheffler's argument against agent-centered restrictions, but Scheffler himself points out the direction that her later defense of such restrictions will follow. That is, Foot must challenge the maximizing conception of rationality presupposed by Scheffler's argument. Scheffler believes that this conception of rationality is a powerful one and is deeply rooted in common sense thinking. But the case of rights suggests that it has its limits—without an alternative conception of rationality, Foot's arguments in favor of agent-centered restrictions seem wanting as she seems to insist on a rationally indefensible bit of common sense. Yet, as we will see in Chapter 6, she does come to offer an alternative conception of rationality.

CHAPTER FIVE

Nonconsequentialism and moral problems

"The operation of benevolence is circumscribed by justice, and even the end which the virtue prescribes is qualified, in that we are not told to be glad that good should come to some when it comes through evil to others." (MD 99)

A defense of common morality

As seen in Chapter 4, Foot rejects utilitarianism as well as other forms of consequentialism. She believes that there are some impermissible actions that produce what utilitarians regard as the best outcome, and some permissible actions that fail to produce such an outcome. Moreover, she denies that there is any way of construing a "best outcome" that would allow us to make sense of widely accepted moral judgments. This motivates her commitment to nonconsequentialism, which is the view that the rightness or wrongness of our actions is not determined solely by the goodness or badness of their consequences.[1] Foot's nonconsequentialism is anchored in her views on virtues; she embraces a traditional conception of the moral virtues in which justice limits the ways in which we can permissibly assist others. In this view, we generally do not act well in violating the rights of an individual in order to bring aid to others. Her work in moral philosophy from the

1980s onward takes on two main tasks, one being a defense of the virtues—how we can rationally understand justice as delimiting benevolent action as well as, at times, demanding extreme sacrifices from individual agents? Answering this question is a special central focus of Foot's late works, which will be discussed in Chapter 6. The other task consists of seeking a rationale for norms of common morality in accordance with the traditional virtues, assuming that they have a justification. "Common morality" is a term Foot uses to refer to widely held moral beliefs that are often at odds with the philosophical "outcome morality" advanced by utilitarians and other consequentialists. For example, Foot thinks that while we regard it as permissible to steer a vehicle away from one person who needs rescuing and who will die without our aid in order to save the lives of five others who need rescuing, we would not think it permissible to deliberately drive over one person, killing him, in order to save five people. In these two cases, the outcome appears to be the same if the five are rescued; yet, the agent's role in bringing about the outcome differs in a way that is morally significant according to common morality. Foot thinks this judgment is widely shared, yet lacks a clear philosophical rationale. She aims to give a rationale for such a judgment, and in doing so, to generate an account of common morality that provides a nonconsequentialist philosophical framework to approach important moral problems.

In this chapter, I will outline Foot's nonconsequentialist approach to moral problems. I begin by explaining her case for two principles she believes to be essential to defend common morality—the Doctrine of Doing and Allowing (DDA) and the Doctrine of Double Effect (DDE). Next, I will discuss Foot's views in relation to one of her most widely discussed hypothetical examples, the Trolley Problem. Finally, to bring the discussion back from the hypothetical realm to real world circumstances, I will discuss the implications of her views on abortion and euthanasia.

Doing and allowing

Intuitively, there is an important moral distinction to be drawn between bringing something about by our own actions and allowing the same to occur. Killing, generally, seems to be worse than letting die; it seems worse to send poisoned food to people in need, thereby ensuring their deaths, than to fail to come to the aid of people who will die of starvation without it. Yet, tying down a rigorous philosophical justification of this distinction proves difficult. In part, this is because the distinction that lies at the heart of common morality is not simply a distinction between what we bring about through our action and what we fail to prevent through inaction. As Foot points out, such a distinction would allow us to manipulate the moral value of our actions in dubious ways. For example, we could install special respirators in hospitals that must be turned on every day to facilitate getting rid of unwanted patients—killing someone by not turning on a respirator would be less bad than killing someone by turning off a normal respirator (MD 89). It is clear, then, that the distinction we are seeking is not a distinction between action and inaction. Instead, Foot proposes that we are looking for a distinction between a causal sequence that we initiate and one that we allow to continue (MD 90). With this distinction, we can provide an analysis of the moral difference between Rescue I, the scenario in which we turn away from saving one drowning person in order to save five, thereby letting the first die, and Rescue II, the scenario in which we must run over one person, killing him, in order to save five others. Rescue II is impermissible because it involves initiating a causal sequence that kills one. Rescue I, by contrast, is permissible because in this scenario, we allow a deadly causal sequence, which we did not initiate, to run its course. This is not to say that all instances of allowing deadly causal sequences to run their courses are permissible, or that the distinction between doing and allowing always makes a difference to the moral status of an action. The claim is only that the distinction sometimes makes a significant moral difference, as it does in this pair of cases.

In Rescue II, if we drive over one person to save five others, the outcome will be the same as the outcome in Rescue I inasmuch as five people will live and one will die. But, clearly, this is an incomplete description of the events, since the rescue of the five in Rescue II requires killing someone. By contrast, in Rescue I, we must let someone die in order to save the five. The one who dies does so as the result of circumstances that we did not create, and this fact is arguably of moral significance. According to Foot, killing is not *per se* worse than letting die; there are, in her view, some instances of letting die that are just as bad as killing. Yet, generally, killing involves the violation of a negative right, a right to noninterference. Letting die generally involves the violation of a positive right, a right to assistance. According to Foot, the former carries precedence over the latter. At the very least, this means that it is generally impermissible to kill one person to save another. Given Foot's views on Rescue II, she clearly endorses a much stronger precedence for negative rights such that it is not permissible to kill one person to save five.[2]

Her view raises the question—why should negative rights have such precedence? For Foot, negative rights take priority as a result of the nature of morality itself—it is not a system of legislation created by a corporate body with a single end in view such as maximizing happiness, but rather, it is a system of compromises arrived at between individuals with different ends (MD 76). In her view, a viable moral system must make a reasonable guarantee of benefits to each person in order to demand conformity to moral rules from all. One of the most important benefits arising from the general observance of moral norms is protection from the threat of being sacrificed whenever it would serve the greater good. This guarantees a "kind of moral space, a space which others are not *allowed* to invade" (MD 103). Elaborating on Foot's rationale for the precedence of negative rights, Warren Quinn points out, "their precedence is essential to the fact of our lives, minds, and bodies really being ours."[3] A moral code that allowed us to harm, kill, or brainwash, so long as doing so would serve the collective good, would not allow us any ownership over our lives or persons; we would be, as Quinn puts it, "cells in a collective whole" rather than genuinely independent persons.[4]

One trouble with this rationale is that it is unclear what level of precedence for negative rights would secure the integrity of the individual. Surely, without minimal precedence forbidding the killing of one to save another, we would live in intolerable fear of being sacrificed for the sake of someone else's well-being. Yet, might not the five persons awaiting rescue reasonably complain that the value of their lives is not being adequately appreciated if we refuse to run over one person to save them? There are two routes to take here—one is to deny that there is any aggregation of value over persons.[5] In that view, it would also be rationally optional to save five in Rescue I, an idea that strikes some as absurd. The second route is to attempt to devise a rationale for a more specific standard. Yet, it is not clear that there is such a standard, and, if so, we may have to stipulate a standard, thereby creating what Foot calls a "contingent principle." And if this is the case, though, we will be entering the questionable territory of applying sanctions in order to uphold conventions that are arbitrary from a moral point of view.[6]

Another problem with Foot's view is that she may fail to avoid the misleading distinction between action and inaction. Foot wants to group together initiation of a causal sequence and keeping the sequence going, and then distinguish these two from allowing the sequence to continue. Yet, what distinguishes keeping a sequence going from allowing it to continue? Intuitively, it seems that one involves action while the other does not, and hence, we are apparently backed into the distinction between action and inaction that Foot wants to avoid.[7] Another problem stems from situations in which we help someone who would not be in danger except for the withdrawal of our assistance. Quinn describes a scenario in which I help an elderly man heat his house with wood. Without my assistance, his home will turn frigid, and he will die. A situation then arises in which five other remote people need my help. Although the situation was not dangerous before, if I help the five, it will become dire for the elderly man through the unanticipated withdrawal of my help. As Quinn puts it, "We might simply stipulate, of course, that any fatal sequence that appears to arise from a *failure* to help someone is really the continuation of a preexisting sequence."[8] Of course, resolving the problem in this way appears to again invoke the rejected distinction between action and inaction.

To respond to these objections, let us return to Foot's concern about respirators that must be turned on every day, a case which I will call "Inverted Respirators." This seems to be an odd choice to illustrate Foot's point about the insufficiency of a distinction between action and inaction, for it is not obvious that her distinction between initiating a causal sequence and allowing one to continue handles the case any better. Am I initiating a causal sequence when I fail to turn on the respirator? It is not clear how failing to turn on the respirator is any more the initiation of a causal sequence than failing to come to the rescue of the one man in Rescue I. It might appear that Foot is appealing to the special obligation that a nurse has to keep the respirator turned on, but if that is the case, our understanding is not being improved by Foot's replacement of the distinction between action and inaction; it is just that the special duties of a nurse makes the obligation to act more stringent. Quinn suggests that we strip away these distracting elements and imagine an Inverted Respirator case in a hospital where the patients pay for their own equipment and staff, and I am an outsider who happens to be on a floor with an electrical problem such that either one patient's respirator functions or those of five other patients. Quinn thinks that it makes a difference whether, in such a circumstance, I must shut the respirator off or keep it turned on. If I must shut the respirator off then my action resembles Rescue II, according to Quinn, and it is impermissible. However, if it is a matter of not turning on a respirator, the situation is more like Rescue I and it is permissible. So, the inverted respirators may indeed make a moral difference.

Still, Quinn may have missed Foot's point. Foot appears to have in mind someone who deliberately sets up inverted respirators so as to "let die," rather than someone who inadvertently walks onto the scene where such respirators have already been set up. Given what she has in mind, the agent is implicated in creating a fatal causal sequence, and thereby the fact that not turning on the respirator involves "inaction" does not affect the moral evaluation of the overall intervention. Presumably, Foot would agree with Quinn's intuitions about the cases he describes. Further, Quinn seems to make another mistake in his discussion of the elderly man. Surely, in such a case, by suddenly removing myself from this situation, I do, in fact, initiate a lethal causal sequence, much as I would if I were driving a train and suddenly decided to stop and jump off to save five people on the side of the track with my medical expertise, while leaving my train to run over one that I could have saved by staying on the train and applying the brakes. Clearly, this case is unlike Rescue I. Although there is a certain description under which my inaction killed the one on the tracks, I did alter my course of action in such a way that I initiate a lethal causal sequence, and so these cases, in fact, both seem more like Rescue II.

Double effect

According to Foot, the DDA alone is insufficient to handle all nonconsequentialist moral intuitions. It must be supplemented with the DDE, according to which our intentions are morally significant, and indeed, can decisively influence our moral evaluation of an action. With the DDE, it may be permissible to do something that has a foreseen though unintended effect, though it would be impermissible to intentionally bring about that effect. For example, in warfare, it is often considered permissible to attack a significant military target, such as a munitions factory, though we foresee that the bombing will kill noncombatants; it would not be permissible to intentionally target those same noncombatants. The latter is an instance of terror bombing, whereas the former is tactical bombing. Although terror bombers usually take pains to maximize casualties, arguably the wrongness of their actions does not depend on their effectiveness in achieving their aims. That is, an act of terror bombing is not worse than an act of tactical bombing only when it is more lethal. According to the DDE, two actions which have equal lethality can differ in their permissibility because of the agent's intentions.

Foot believes that this principle is necessary because the DDA does not cover some morally significant distinctions. For example, consider a case in which we possess a certain drug, but only enough to either cure one person suffering from a fatal condition, or to save five others who are suffering from a milder, though still fatal case of the same illness. In such a circumstance, we can permissibly give the drug to the five who are suffering from the milder form of the disease. If we could save all six, we would surely do so. Clearly, we do not intend the death of the one, though we foresee it as a consequence of our actions. However, it is not permissible to withhold a live-saving drug from one in order to use his organs to save the lives of the five others after he dies. In this case, the death of the one is an essential means to the achievement of the end, and so his death is strictly intended. Although I am allowing someone to die and not perpetrating a killing by my own agency, what I do is impermissible. Only the DDE captures the distinction between these cases and it is therefore an important complement to the DDA. The DDE is also important to the evaluation of persons for Foot. Just as it would be wrong to withhold a drug from one in order to use his organs to save others, it would likewise be objectionable to be glad of someone's death because his organs could then be used to save five (MD 92). Still, the DDE cannot stand on its own, according to Foot—we need both the DDE and the DDA. That is because we can sometimes impermissibly initiate harm with indirect intention. She gives the example of wicked merchants who knowingly sell poisoned oil—their intention is not to harm their customers, but only to turn a profit; yet, they are clearly initiating a harmful causal sequence.

Likewise, the DDA rules out manufacturing a drug that would help five when doing so would release a toxic substance that would kill one. Although the death of the one is not a means to saving the five, and it is not directly intended, it is still something that I cause in the manufacture of the drug, and it is, therefore, ruled out by the DDA.

Although Foot in her later work embraces the DDE as a central component of nonconsequentialist moral thinking, her earlier paper, "The Problem of Abortion and the Doctrine of Double Effect" (1967), criticizes the doctrine. Her central objection in that paper is that it does not handle cases such as the manufacture of the drug previously mentioned. Obviously, she came to realize that the DDE need not cover all cases, and that the DDA and DDE can be viewed as complementary moral principles. However, in this article, she raises and sets aside an issue that has come to seem considerably more difficult for advocates of the DDE—the so-called "problem of closeness." The issue here is how to discern what an agent strictly intends, which is crucial for applying the DDE. Consider a pair of cases involving abortion. In the first case, a craniotomy must be performed on a fetus in order to extract it from the mother, who would otherwise die. In the second case, a woman needs a hysterectomy to save her life, but she is pregnant and the procedure will kill the fetus. Advocates of the doctrine of double effect who affirm the moral rights of fetuses have held that the hysterectomy is permissible, but the craniotomy is not. The death of the fetus is a means to saving the life of the mother in the craniotomy case and, therefore, the surgeon strictly intends it and this is not allowed. However, the death of the fetus is not a means to saving the woman in the hysterectomy case, since the life-saving procedure could be performed without the involvement of the fetus, and therefore, it is not strictly intended. An objection to this view is that it is unclear that the craniotomy case involves the strict intention to kill the fetus; the surgeon only aims to make its head smaller, and if the surgeon could do so without killing the fetus, he surely would. As Jonathan Bennett has argued, something similar could be said about the terror bomber case. The terror bomber's aim is presumably to demoralize the population so that they will be willing to capitulate, and to achieve this end, he does not need the civilians to actually die—he only needs them to *appear* dead.[9] So, either some clearer criterion of what one strictly intends must be offered, or else the DDE offers us no guidance.

Although Foot's later defense of the principle of the DDE did not take on this objection, the principle is so central to Foot's nonconsequentialism that we should consider whether it can be defended. One approach, taken by Warren Quinn, is to revise the DDE in such a way that it rules out intentionally involving others in a foreseeably harmful event to further one's purpose. The terror bomber intends an explosion that will foreseeably cause the deaths of many civilians, and those deaths (or apparent deaths) further his purpose. The tactical bomber, by contrast, intends an explosion that he foresees will cause the deaths of civilians, but those deaths are irrelevant to his purpose. The harm caused by the involvement need not be useful and the usefulness of the involvement need not be causally connected with the harm in any especially close way.[10] Quinn thereby sidesteps the issue raised by Bennett.[11]

Judith Jarvis Thomson and Thomas Scanlon have raised another issue for the DDE, including Quinn's revised formulation of it. The DDE would have us appeal to the agent's intention in deciding on the permissibility of an action, and this, they think, is clearly absurd. Thomson discusses the case of a doctor who injects a patient in unbearable suffering with a lethal dose of painkillers. Some advocates of the DDE have held that it is permissible to inject, provided that the doctor's intention is to alleviate the suffering rather than to kill the patient. Regarding this reasoning, Thomson writes:

> According to [the DDE], the question whether it is morally permissible for the doctor to inject a lethal drug turns on whether the doctor would be doing so intending death or only intending relief from pain . . . If the only available doctor would inject to cause the patient's death, or is incapable of becoming clear enough about her own intentions to conclude that what she intends is *only* to relieve the patient's pain, then—according to [the DDE]—the doctor may not proceed, and the patient must therefore continue to suffer. That cannot be right.[12]

Scanlon, concurring with Thomson, proposes the following thought experiment:

> Suppose you were prime minister, and the commander of the air force described to you a planned air raid that would be expected to destroy a munitions plant and kill a certain number

of civilians . . . If he asked you whether you thought this was morally permissible, you would not say, "Well, that depends on what your intention would be in carrying it out. Would you intend to kill the civilians, or would their deaths be merely unintended but foreseeable (albeit beneficial) side effect of the destruction of the plant?"[13]

More generally, Thomson and Scanlon argue that the appeal of the DDE lies in confusion—those who embrace the DDE fail to recognize seriously enough the distinction between the permissibility of an action and what an action reveals about an individual's moral character. A morally permissible action can still be bad *qua* action and reveal an agent's character as bad, or at least that the deliberation leading up to an individual action was flawed.

The confusion that worries Thomson and Scanlon cannot be attributed to Foot, as she explicitly acknowledges the distinction between permissibility and other moral evaluations of acts and persons (MD 91–2). Nevertheless, Thomson and Scanlon may have a point about the irrelevance of intention to permissibility. The implausibility of the applications of the DDE envisaged by Thomson and Scanlon stems from the way in which permissibility would depend on something subjective. When we speak about the permissibility of an action, we are clearly not talking about anything subjective; yet, perhaps they are misled in taking intention to be something subjective. Anscombe, in her writing on double effect, noticed this issue and called attention to what she regarded as a mistaken Cartesian psychology, according to which "intention was an interior act of the mind which could be produced at will" (ERP 59). Anscombe contends that it is not entirely up to the agent to define his intention in acting, noting that, "the greater number of things which you would say straight off a man did or was doing, will be things he intends."[14] We readily attribute actions to other people, and that requires attributing to them more than mere bodily movements. From the nature and context of a person's bodily movements, we are able to ascertain that a person is doing something with knowledge of what they are doing and, generally, we get it right. Yet, a person's own understanding plays some role in defining what they are doing and, at times, we mistake what a person is doing by misjudging her aims. Nevertheless, a person is not doing just whatever they say they are doing; some claims about intention could disqualify an individual from consideration as a competent agent. So, while there is a subjective component to intentions that is relevant to the definition of a person's action, there is a limited range of possible intentions for a competent agent to possess in any given context.

Yet, there are still more decisive considerations to bring against the argument of Thomson and Scanlon. Let us imagine that we were faced with a doctor who indeed wanted to see a patient dead, whether out of sheer sadism or other self-serving motive, and not out of the desire to relieve his pain. It is not as clear as Thomson would have us believe that we would allow such a doctor near any patients, even one suffering from a terminal illness. Likewise, in Scanlon's example, we should find it alarming if, as the prime minister of a country with an air force, the commander of such military strength were out to spill civilian blood. The absurdity of the question, as posed by Scanlon, stems from the fact that we do not ordinarily need to ask what our aim is in performing an action; it should be clear that our aim is to take out a munitions factory, if such a plan is under discussion. There *might* be some question if it is the case that a particular air force commander's past actions and decisions raise concerns about a potential cruel or callous streak in his character. In that case, it would not sound so odd to question whether he is creating a pretext to shed blood, though one probably would not use the language that Scanlon puts in the mouth of his hypothetical prime minister.

A possible rejoinder here for Thomson and Scanlon is that, in both instances, intention matters only because of its predictive value; that is, we might be averse to allowing people who express morally objectionable intentions to perform certain actions because people acting with such intention are more likely to do harm. This is a rejoinder because it would mean that intention has no moral significance *per se*. Yet, it is not evidently the case that our concern is solely with the potential for a worse outcome. We might find the actions impermissible because when acting with such intentions, the agents would be doing something atrocious; that is, they would be doing wrong, whatever the outcome. Recall that, for Foot, our moral codes are comprised of rules and aims. In formulating a moral code, we abstract from the character of the agents performing deeds in order to posit rules that specify prohibitions and duties for types of actions. Questions of permissibility typically arise in reflecting on our moral code. Permissibility in relation to our moral code is a matter of which actions are allowed and which ends we are allowed to target. Yet, permissibility is not necessarily exhausted by our moral code. We may find actions performed with certain motives and intentions morally objectionable, whereas a similar action done by someone with different motives would be acceptable. The question then is not whether it is permissible to φ, which pertains, not to a *type* of acting considered in abstraction from the motives of the agent, but to whether *this act of* φ-ing is permissible, taking a concrete action done by a particular agent. The DDE is not a rule in our moral code, but a doctrine or principle that helps guide our judgment in determining whether an individual act is permissible. To return to Thomson's example, if we had to cast about desperately for a physician who lacked any questionable motives to use a lethal injection of painkiller, we may allow considerations of a patient in extreme pain to override concerns about the fact that a man is aiming at securing the death of someone. The doctor commits murder, and thereby does something morally objectionable, but all things considered, we may decide to allow it, given that it is the only way to alleviate unbearable suffering.

A final issue for the DDE concerns its rationale. Foot appears to think that the precedence of negative rights provides a rationale for the DDE as well as the DDA, and again, Quinn elaborates on this idea. The intuitive idea is that the precedence of negative rights generally makes it impermissible to intentionally violate someone's negative rights. Still, we might wonder whether there is any comfort in knowing that such rights were not violated intentionally. In other words, do those who stand to be killed by a tactical bomber have any less reason to complain of the danger to their lives than those who stand to be killed by a terror bomber? Quinn thinks that someone who harms by direct agency takes up a distinct attitude toward the victim that involves regarding someone "as if they were then and there *for* his purposes."[15] Yet, those harmed by indirect agency are not regarded as such because they are not essential to the agent's purposes. That is, the terror bomber's plan essentially involves the victims involuntarily, whereas the tactical bomber's plan only incidentally involves others involuntarily. If civilians were not present, the tactical bombers plans would still be successful. The impact on these victims is not lessened, of course; however, if my argument is correct, the attitude of an agent involved in the execution of a particular action can sometimes make a difference as to whether or not it is permissible. Harmful actions involving direct agency are, in Quinn's view, worse in some degree than harmful actions involving indirect agency. Clearly, this distinction does not always amount to a difference of permissibility, but according to proponents of the DDE, it has the potential to do just that.

The trolley problem

In "The Problem of Abortion and the Doctrine of Double Effect," Foot raises a case that has been the subject of much subsequent discussion—a runaway trolley is headed toward five people who will be killed by the collision, but it could be steered onto a track on which there is only one person (VV 23). Intuitively, it seems permissible to turn the trolley to hit and kill one person, but the problem is that it does not seem permissible to kill one to save five in cases such as Rescue II or Transplant. Why, Foot asks, can we not argue for the permissibility of killing one to save five in those cases by appealing to the Trolley case? As we have seen, Foot argues that negative rights are generally stronger than positive rights, and she argues in "The Problem of Abortion" that this helps us answer the Trolley Problem. In Rescue II and Transplant, we must violate someone's negative rights in order to meet the positive rights of others, and this is impermissible because the negative rights have a precedence over the positive rights that is not outweighed by five people's need for assistance. In Trolley, by contrast, we are not violating negative rights in order to meet positive rights; the situation pits the negative rights of the five against the negative rights of one, and both choices involve violating someone's negative rights. In such a case, it seems clearly preferable to minimize the violation of negative rights by turning the trolley. Yet, as Judith Jarvis Thomson has shown, this solution does not hold for a close variant of Trolley, which she calls "Bystander at the Switch."[16] In this case, the runaway trolley's driver has collapsed from panic, but there is a bystander with a switch who can do nothing and allow five to die, or pull the switch and divert the trolley toward the one. Thomson argues that the bystander (unlike the driver) would not be killing if he does nothing, but kills if he does pull the switch. In any case, Thomson thinks that it is clearly permissible to pull the switch in this situation—a view that goes against both the idea that killing is worse than letting die, and that negative rights always trump positive rights.

Another possible rationale for drawing a distinction between Trolley/Bystander and Rescue II/Transplant is that the impermissible cases involve treating some people as a mere means. In other words, the permissibility of Trolley and Bystander could be explained by the DDE, since in both cases, the one is not a means to saving the five, and so the death of the one is not strictly intended by the person turning the trolley. Thomson ingeniously disarms this rationale as well, for she points out that one could easily convert Bystander into a case where the one is a means to saving the five without changing the permissibility of turning the trolley. Imagine that a loop is added to the track, so that turning the trolley will direct it away from the five and make it begin a loop. Eventually, the trolley would come around the loop and threaten the five from the other direction, but fortunately there is one person on the track, and if the trolley hits him, it will come to a stop before hitting the five. Thomson thinks that turning the trolley in this case would be permissible, even though now, the one is a necessary means to saving the five. According to her, what makes turning the trolley permissible in all of these cases is that a "distributive exemption" to negative rights applies to all of them. This exemption allows us to divert a preexisting threat so that it kills fewer people than it would otherwise, when doing so would not involve a "gross impingement" on the rights of the few.[17] So, for example, this exemption would not allow one to push a man standing on a bridge over the trolley and onto the track in order to stop the trolley, because that act itself involves a violation of the individual's rights—it creates a lethal sequence that did not previously exist and as such involves a gross impingement on the individual's rights. In cases covered by the distributive exemption, the victims are already exposed to some threat by being on the tracks, and do not have a right against having the preexisting threat directed at them for the sake of saving a greater number, or so Thomson argues, and Foot endorses this argument (MD 85).

A remaining issue here is that Loop appears to pose a counterexample to the DDE. After all, it is a case in which one is killed as an essential means to attaining a good end, and it is permissible, in Thomson's view, at least. The distributive exemption allows a preexisting threat to be redirected, but it is supposed to be a rather conservative exemption inasmuch as it requires us to otherwise respect the rights of those against whom the threat is directed. That is, the exemption is limited to the redirection of the preexisting threat. Frances Kamm has argued that Loop does not pose a counter-example to the DDE because it is not true that a rational agent intends the means to his ends. She thinks that although the bystander would not redirect the trolley onto the loop unless the one were there to stop the trolley and thereby save the five, the bystander does not necessarily intend the death of the one. Kamm believes that a common test for intention—the counterfactual test— is flawed.[18] According to the counterfactual test, if an agent will only do something provided it has a certain effect, then one intends that effect. In this case, the bystander only turns the trolley on the assumption that it will hit the one, bringing it to a stop and thereby saving the five. As Kamm puts it, "the test fails to distinguish effects the belief in which is a condition of action from effects that are intended."[19] In her view, there is a general distinction that is often ignored between doing something only because a certain effect will thereby be realized and doing it in order to realize that effect. Hence, in Kamm's view, there is also room for unintended, yet necessary effects of one's action, that is, means to the achievement of one's end that are not intended.

Abortion and euthanasia

So far, the discussion has ranged over many highly artificial thought experiments, and so, it may seem that we are discussing what Quinn calls "the morality of public transportation."[20] Still, Foot aims to use such thought experiments to sharpen our unreflective intuitions and focus our attention on implications of commonly held principles in order to generate insights for real life cases, including abortion and euthanasia. Foot is skeptical of any attempt to resolve the abortion debate without settling the issue of whether and when the fetus has moral rights, and she regards this as an intractable issue (MD 87). In this view, she takes sides against Thomson, who argued that some abortions are permissible even if we allow for the sake of argument that the fetus has full moral status. Thomson argues by analogy— imagine that while we sleep, a group of music lovers stealthily attach to us a famous violinist who is suffering from an ailment, and we uniquely can keep him alive for roughly nine months, as he convalesces.[21] The question is—may we detach the violinist, causing his death? Thomson argues that we may, since our negative rights have been violated and no one has the right to use another's body, even to save his own life. Of course, the analogy here is limited to cases of nonconsensual impregnation, such as those resulting from rape.

Foot argues that the analogy has a devastating fault. There is a morally significant difference between unhooking someone from one's own body, which does not involve initiating a fatal causal sequence, since the person was already in the grips of a fatal condition before being hooked up to us, and abortion, which does initiate a fatal sequence. Foot believes that this makes abortion seem like Rescue II, whereas the unhooking of the violinist is like Rescue I. As Foot puts it, "the fetus is not in jeopardy because it is in its mother's womb; it is merely dependent on her in the way children are dependent on their parents for food" (MD 87). Yet, this does not seem entirely true, as children are dependent on their parents for food in a way that they can be fed by others, whereas the same is not true of pre-term fetuses, and this is what creates the special restriction on the rights of the mother, at least in cases of pregnancies resulting from rape. Still, Foot has a point that there is a disanalogy inasmuch as a healthy fetus in a healthy mother is not under a threat unless starting an abortion procedure creates one.

Foot's considered position on abortion, then, seems to be that the moral community must decide whether or not to count the fetus as a human being (MD 7). Yet, as I argued above, this position is an unhappy one and we should be reticent to embrace it. If we include fetuses in the moral community, a penalty of law would have to apply to those who kill them, and surely, punishment should not be dealt on the basis of an arbitrary stipulation if it can be avoided. As Rosalind Hursthouse has argued, the notion of "moral status" may be leading us astray here. The morality of the treatment of fetuses may not be a simple matter of determining whether it is included or excluded from the community of persons. Rather, it may be a matter of looking at the value of parenting and childbearing within the context of human life. Some abortions clearly fail to respect the value of parenting and fail to take human life seriously; others, such as an abortion performed on a frightened child impregnated by rape or incest, may yet respect that value.[22] Foot looks at the issue of abortion from the perspective of justice and charity. In her view, the only way that the issue can be resolved is to decide whether the fetus deserves the protection of justice. Hursthouse asks us to consider the issue from the perspective of other virtues—we must avoid being light-minded and callous about pregnancy and parenting, and hence exhibit appropriate seriousness and consideration for the goods at stake in deciding whether or not to abort. In a similar vein, I have argued that our notion of justice might be too narrow, and that a wider conception of justice could include creatures and things that are not persons.[23] These approaches are inspired by Foot, but attempt to take a wider view of the resources at the disposal of a virtue-based approach to moral problems.

Perhaps Foot's most penetrating article on moral problems is her "Euthanasia" (1977). Foot defines euthanasia as a killing that is for the good of the individual in question, and she asks whether such an act can ever be permissible. One central question here is whether it can ever be good for an individual to be deprived of his life, and hence, one of Foot's central purposes is to determine what sort of a good life is for a person. She rejects the narrowly hedonistic view that the value of life is determined by the balance of pleasure versus pain it promises. In her view, life is often still a good to someone who is suffering and who is likely to continue in such a state. Yet, she also argues that merely being alive without suffering is not a good (VV 42). What is of value, in her view, is the ordinary human life that contains at least a minimum of "basic human goods," which include—"that a man is not driven to work far beyond his capacity; that he has the support of a family or community; that he can more or less satisfy his hunger; that he has hopes for the future; that he can lie down to rest at night" (Ibid.). In the absence of such minimal goods, she argues that life is not a good to a person.

The issue of the permissibility of euthanasia for Foot, then, turns to issues about justice and charity (VV 44). In her view, even when it seems better for someone not to survive, we must respect that person's rights. Hence, for her, involuntary active euthanasia can never be permissible. However, the right to assistance in staying alive calls upon the charity of others and not justice, except in the case of a doctor who has a contractual duty to help keep us alive. Yet, even in the case of a doctor, where assistance is a matter of justice, our claim to that assistance is limited by the claims of others as well as a regard for our well-being. That is, there may come a point at which such "assistance" as a doctor can offer to prolong a patient's life does not actually confer any benefit, and in such a case, it is not contrary to justice or charity for the doctor to withhold treatment; as Foot points out, such instances of passive euthanasia are already widely practiced (VV 56). However, she argues that it may be justified not to prolong the life of someone who wants to live, giving the example of a dying soldier whose life could be prolonged with a certain drug, but who would thereby face death by starvation. According to Foot, nonvoluntary passive euthanasia is permissible in such an instance.

Of course, the central controversy here is whether voluntary active euthanasia is permissible. She dismisses James Rachels' claim that if we permit passive euthanasia, then the only consistent position is to permit active euthanasia in similar circumstances because it is "more humane" than passive euthanasia.[24] Foot argues by analogy that it may be "more humane" to deprive someone of property that brings evil to him, but nevertheless, taking it away would be contrary to justice (VV 50). However, someone may give permission for the destruction of his property, and as Foot concludes, "If someone gives you permission to destroy his property it can no longer be said that you have no right to do so, and I do not see why it should not be the same with taking a man's life" (VV 53). Nevertheless, Foot admits that the moral issue is not entirely resolved by the matter of rights, so it does not follow that there is no moral objection to doing something because it would involve no violation of rights. It is then a matter of whether it would be good for the person to die and, hence, whether it would be contrary to charity. This rules out cases in which death is wished for by someone who is facing a life of dependency because they are worried about being a burden on others. In such circumstances, other things being equal, the death would not be for the good of the person.

Foot also has concerns about the practice of euthanasia that make her hesitate in suggesting that the practice ought to be more widely legalized. As is generally acknowledged, there is much room for the abuse of euthanasia in the pursuit of cutting expenses and burdens. Yet, even aside from such issues, there is a case to be made, I believe, that Foot's exclusive focus on justice and charity blinkers her view of the morality of euthanasia. Consider again Foot's comparison of life with property. Her treatment of property takes a univocal view of property, but not all property is the same.

Say I own a precious piece of art, a singular masterpiece. Legally speaking, my ownership of the work gives me the right to dispose of it as I please. But clearly, that consideration does not exhaust the moral issues regarding my treatment of the piece. It may be said that I owe it to others to preserve a piece of art for its historical and cultural importance, and I would say that wantonly destroying such a thing is objectionable even apart from such considerations. A virtuous agent would show some degree of respect for such an object. Likewise, one might say that if we compare life to property, as something over which we exercise rights in our control of the thing, these rights are not without some moral constraints. Surely, if life is to be compared with property, it is more like a precious painting than a valueless knick-knack that could be thrown aside when it no longer serves one's interests. There is, arguably, an issue of respect for life that goes beyond justice and charity. Though this value does not necessarily rule out voluntary active euthanasia, it is arguably another factor, beyond justice and charity, to be weighed in the consideration of when such an action might be permissible.

CHAPTER SIX

Human nature and virtue

"Good rules, including moral codes, are not mere conventions but things that are needed in human life. And only incorrect moral judgments (such as the belief that there is nothing wrong with slavery, or that homoerotic behavior is 'wrong') deserve to be downgraded as 'mere opinion,' and contrasted with that which has its basis in nature." (RG 11)

Foot's fresh start

In her final published essay, "Rationality and Goodness" (2004), Foot discusses the case of a farm boy from the Sudetenland who chose to die rather than to serve the Nazis.[1] In a letter to his family, he writes, "We did not sign up for the SS, and so they condemned us to death. Both of us would rather die than stain our consciences with such deeds of horror" (RG 2).[2] With regard to this situation, Foot asks, "Was this a rational choice? On what theory of practical rationality – of the rationality of choices – can this be made out?" (RG 2).

In posing this question, Foot returns to a theme of her earliest work in moral philosophy—how moral considerations give us reasons. She believes that she has found a new approach that shows the Sudetenland boy's choice to be rational, and that it would be rational for any similarly situated human agent to make that choice. This constitutes a second reversal of her view on this subject—in her early writings, Foot argues that all rational agents would necessarily have reason to be moral as the virtues are essential for human beings to attain the benefit of fulfilling species-typical desires (see Chapter 2). Hence, in her early period, Foot embraces a sort of moral rationalism, which is the view that moral reasons inevitably give us reasons for action. As shown in Chapter 3, Foot changes her mind concerning this view; she comes to think that the extreme demands that virtue can impose on us undermine her earlier attempt to justify the virtues by way of appealing to their benefits. In her middle period, then, Foot argues against moral rationalism. She thinks moral philosophers wrongly embrace the assumption that moral demands must be understood as categorical demands, which means that they apply to all agents, regardless of their desires. She believes this assumption obscures our reasons for doing things that require considerable sacrifice, such as the choice made by the Sudetenland boy. The correct explanation of his motivation, as she argues in her middle period, is that as a morally good person, he has a particularly strong desire to do what is just and to avoid injustice. She embraces the idea that those without such desires have no reason to be moral.

In her late period, however, she reverses her thoughts once again on this issue. She now believes that she erred in her middle period by embracing an erroneous view of reasons for action. Because considerations become reasons through a connection with an agent's desires, her middle period view falls into a category of instrumentalist theories of reasons for action. In such views, genuine reasons for action advance the fulfillment of our desires or our interests. These views are open to a serious objection that was pointed out by Warren Quinn, who argues that with such instrumentalist conceptions of reasons for action, we can be rationally shameless. These views tell us that an agent is rational when she acts on reasons that maximize the fulfillment of her preferences or interests, and it bids us to do that without regard to their content. The consequence of this view is that those with nasty preferences are adviced by such views of practical rationality to maximize the fulfillment of those preferences.[3] This sits awkwardly with the idea that rationality is something that is supposed to guide our action.

Foot proposes that we reject the demand that moral actions fit with a preconceived notion of practical rationality, and instead, we ought to adopt the view that moral reasons are one set of reasons among others to which a rational agent must respond (NG 11). After all, as Quinn points out, practical rationality is held to be an authoritative guide to action as well as a virtue, and so, surely, practical rationality must require an agent to take account of the moral features of ends. Whether or not practical rationality requires taking account of those features is clearly pertinent to whether it is a genuine virtue, much less a master virtue. This argument suggests that our standards of rationality should derive from our standards of goodness of the will, rather than the other way around. In this view, our conception of practical rationality must fit within our overall conception of the human good. Foot believes that we can see such an approach at work in the way we reject present-desire theories of reasons for action. We commonly think that someone who puts her future at risk for the sake of some trivial, transient desire is behaving foolishly. As Foot writes, "Being unable to fit the supposed 'reason' into some preconceived present-desire-based theory of reasons for action, we do not query whether it really is a foolish way to behave, but rather hang onto the evaluation and shape our theory of reasons accordingly" (NG 63).

Moral reasons are of course not the only reasons to which we must respond to be rational agents. Foot believes that moral considerations, such as those of justice and charity, are on par with self-interest and desire-fulfillment. She also believes that there are considerations of family and friendship that provide a separate category of reasons for action (RG 8–9). A judgment about what is practically rational requires weighing these various considerations, and she concludes, "It is not always rational to give help where it is needed, to keep a promise, or even . . . always to speak the truth" (NG 11). Hence, moral reasons are not overriding. For example, a soldier may lie to save himself when in the hands of an enemy (RG 7). Even considerations of desire fulfillment can trump moral considerations, as, for example, an insignificant promise may be overridden by an unexpected opportunity to fulfill a long-held desire.

In the case of the Sudetenland farm boy, the result of Foot's view is that we need not demonstrate that his decision to embrace death rather than serve the Nazis is in his best interest or serves his strongest desires. Of course, there is a certain sense in which he would rather die than serve the Nazis, but, as Foot points out, he need not lack a very strong desire to live for his action to count as rational. As she writes, "If, according to a particular theory of rationality, a good action such as his seems dubiously rational, then so much the worse, not for the judgment, but rather for the theory" (RG 6).

She returns to the view that there are different sets of considerations that have the ability to justify and explain actions. In her early work, Foot apparently appeals to intuitions about what we count as reasons for action, though in her late work, she adds to this account a framework for assessing which considerations possess this independent rationalizing status. She believes that the human will must be assessed against the background of facts concerning human life, especially against facts about what humans need. As Foot puts it, "the evaluation of human action depends . . . on essential features of specifically human life" (NG 14). In Foot's view, then, our conception of practical rationality is inevitably tied to what is good for human beings, and must answer to facts concerning what is good for human beings as a species. We must take certain facts about the human condition into account and then we will see that these facts provide the basis for a case in favor of virtues, including, most importantly for Foot, justice and charity.

Natural norms and human goodness

The second central idea of Foot's late work is that moral goodness is a form of what she calls "natural goodness." That is, moral goodness is an aspect of what makes us good as human beings. In this idea, she develops a strain of thought present in some of her early writings such as "Goodness and Choice," where she defends the idea that there are objective features of living things that make them good as members of their species. She argues against Hare that there is a sense of "good cactus" that is not merely a matter of preferences that we have in cacti—there are features of a good cactus that depend on what it is to flourish as a cactus (VV 141). That is, a blighted, damaged, or otherwise unhealthy cactus is not, in this sense, a good cactus. This notion of "natural goodness" is developed in her late work, where she claims that virtue makes humans good in the same way that blight-free, lush green flesh in a certain shape makes a cactus good. The norms that determine what makes something a good member of its kind, she calls "natural norms."

In *Natural Goodness*, Foot makes the claim that natural norms are essential to the identification of anything as an organism—to identify something as an organism is *ipso facto* to view it from a normative standpoint. We can look at an organism as an ordinary physical system, but to do so is to miss its biological nature. There are two premises to her argument for this point—first, grasping something as an organism requires us to situate the organism against the background of its species, and second, to situate an organism against the background of its species requires us to consider it from a normative perspective. Let us look at the first premise. According to Michael Thompson, whose work on living things provides the basis for Foot's account, identifying something as an organism situates it within a "wider context," which is its kind. As Thompson puts it, "If a thing is alive, if it is an *organism*, then some particular vital operations and processes must go on in it from time to time – eating, budding out, breathing, walking, growing, thinking, photosynthesizing."[4] But nothing can fall under these descriptions when understood only in terms appropriate to a nonliving physical thing. Consider, for example, the case of eating—for an organism to be regarded as eating something, one must take it to be ingesting that which is normally nutritious for its kind, as well as absorbing it in such a way as to derive nutrition from it. Otherwise, we could not say that we witnessed an organism eating something, but instead, we would be observing a fortuitous occurrence whereby an organism takes in some sort of material which happens to further its life.[5] Only against the background of a life form, which determines a background of norms for understanding the doings of an instance of that form of life, can the activities of an organism be understood as eating, or performing any other vital activity.[6]

From this account, we can see that all living things exhibit, in various ways, a special kind of agency.[7] The growth of a fern is essentially different from the growth of a nonliving thing such as puddle of rainwater or a trash heap, as the fern brings about its own growth by a process of cell division. Also, we can provide a description of how such a process should advance, and recognize when it has gone awry, whereas there is no question of the growth of a trash heap going wrong. The growth of a fern differs from that of a rhododendron, even though they both exhibit the same sort of agency characteristic of living things. We must, in principle, be able to discern the growth *of* the fern from a growth *on* the fern that is due to blight, for example, and such discernment requires a conception of how the fern's life should progress. Hence, the vital operations that characterize something as an organism are intelligible only against the background of a life form. A particular organism, then, is understandable only in its relation to its species and how an individual of that species characteristically lives; hence, it involves a rudimentary identification of the thing as functionally organized. Note that this is a logical claim about what is involved in identifying something as an organism; the existence of life forms, in the sense employed by Thompson, is not a contingent fact about the development of the present set of living organisms, as is the existence of genera and of phyla. The existence of a life form is presupposed whenever we identify anything as an organism, be it the first or the last of its kind.

The second premise in Foot's argument is again—to situate an organism against the background of the characteristic function of its kind is to consider it from a normative perspective. More precisely, it is to assess that organism against what is normal for organisms of its species, and in doing so, we make a normative assessment. Of course, there are many variations that are possible within a species, and not every variation found in an individual will count as a defect. As Foot points out, a blue tit can lack the patch of blue on its head without being hindered in living its life; this lack is not, then, a defect (NG 30). So, natural normativity involves some recognition of the specific components that are crucial to carrying out an organism's vital operations. We must note that to possess such insight, we merely need to appreciate that the organism is functionally organized, which is precisely what occurs when we situate an organism against the background of its species. This further implies that to consider an organism as such involves some recognition (though possibly mistaken) of its needs.

As we have seen, to characterize something as possessing the agency distinctive of living things requires bringing to bear norms for the life form of that individual; this is no less true in our own case. Of course, humans are capable of various modes of living, and in light of such diversity, it is questionable whether there is any characteristically human life, and so, whether there is any univocal sense of "good human." Foot acknowledges that humans are rational animals and she believes this characteristic introduces a "sea change" in how we approach describing our own species; reasoning and the application of reasoning to action are features that are evaluated in human beings. As Foot writes, "[W]hile [non-human] animals go for the good (thing) *that they see,* human beings go for *what they see as good*" (NG 56). We are capable of responding to reasons in a distinctively explicit way, inasmuch as we act on some understanding of which things are good. In fact, it is precisely the application of reasoning to our action that interests us in ethical evaluation. Foot claims that vices are defects in our responsiveness to reasons for action, which constitutes a sort of natural defect in humans, and, specifically, individuals with vices have defective wills. Inasmuch as we have the capacity to reason about how to act, we are subject to a distinctive sort of evaluation; unlike other natural defects, which may simply be the result of bad luck, we are responsible for our conception of how to act, and therefore can answer to rational criticism of that conception.

Thus far, this view appears to build the foundations of ethics on the very general characteristic of rationality, leaving aside other aspects of our nature. If so, it will surely not advance the project of justifying the virtues, for such a view seems to lead us to the empty standard of acting in accordance with "right reason." Yet, as pointed out above, the appeal to human nature serves not only to *tell us that we are rational*, but also to *define what it is to reason well*. NeoAristotelian ethical naturalism, as Foot pursues it, must be understood as a thesis concerning rationality, according to which, practical rationality is species-relative. Our reasoning cannot ignore what we need as human beings and yet still claim to exhibit practical rationality. Hence, Foot can claim that as rational animals we are freed from a certain kind of obedience to nature, while maintaining that nature has some normative role for us; nature is normative over our reasoning, but not directly over our action. Foot states that human beings strive for what we see as good rather than the good that we see, as nonhuman animals do; she adds that what we see as good is inevitably informed by a conception of our form of life. Making that conception explicit and subjecting it to criticism is an essential part of moral reform, for ethical naturalists.

Biology and naturalism for rational animals

Despite the diversity of lives that we can choose, Foot argues that human beings are vulnerable to deprivations that parallel natural defects found in plants and animals. For example, human beings need the mental capacity for learning language, understanding stories, joining in songs, and laughing at jokes (NG 43). Foot writes:

> In spite of the diversity of human goods—the elements that can make up good human lives—it is therefore possible that the concept of a good human life plays the same part in determining goodness of human characteristics and operations that the concept of nourishing plays in the determination of goodness in plants and animals. So far the conceptual structure seems to be intact. (NG 44)

However, it is important to realize that Foot is not saying that our understanding of good human reasoning is to be based on a morally neutral, biological notion of flourishing. There is a straightforward misreading of Foot's naturalism that misconstrues what is *natural* about Foot's naturalism, a misreading exemplified in Chrisoula Andreou's "Getting On in a Varied World."[8] She interprets Foot as arguing that moral goodness is crucial for human survival and reproduction. In Andreou's reading, Foot is subject to criticisms that arise from none too recent work in empirical biology. First, there is reason to think that we could reproduce successfully by adopting strategies such as those common in some birds; that is, under difficult conditions, we could kill off weaker children so we could invest more energy in the stronger children. Such a strategy is immoral, as Andreou rightly argues, but she cannot see how such mixed sound natural types are ruled out by Foot's naturalism, and hence she believes Foot simply fails to recognize the possibility of these strategies. Likewise, we could find type differentiation in human beings; there could be a certain prevalence of psychopaths among us without interfering with a well-functioning society (apparently, this is not merely hypothetical, as roughly 1 per cent of the general population is psychopathic with 4 per cent of corporate CEOs suffering from the condition). Again, the existence of multiple sound natural types is a possibility that is not ruled out by Foot's views. Mixed sound natural types and multiple sound natural types are both widely exhibited in nature, and Foot, in her ignorance of empirical biology, overlooks them, and thus her theory founders because of it, at least according to Andreou.

But Andreou overlooks crucial aspects of Foot's view, demonstrating that it is not, in fact, vulnerable to these criticisms. Foot argues that ethical naturalism need not define the aim of practical reasoning in terms of promoting survival and reproduction, and she explicitly claims that she is not doing so. Rather, she believes that we inevitably possess an understanding of what makes for a good human life that informs our understanding of good human reasoning, and good human character in general. *Structurally*, this is how the parts of a plant are deemed good with reference to the flourishing of a plant. But Foot does not mean to suggest that the *content* of norms of governing human reasoning and character must be pegged to a notion of lush-green-leaves-and-deep-roots flourishing as adapted to human terms. Certainly, there are norms governing our assessment of human health, but there are also norms specifying how events are supposed to proceed when we reason and act, and these norms cannot be equated with what promotes human health, survival or reproduction, except insofar as these are rationally chosen by humans. We do not hold survival and reproduction as sacrosanct values, and therefore, it is not always rationally chosen. We see this reflected by the fact that justice and other virtues may require us to forgo having children, or even to lay down our lives. Foot clearly has these points in mind when she says, "Lack of capacity to reproduce is a defect in a human being. But choice of childlessness and even celibacy is not thereby shown to be defective choice, because human good is not the same as plant or animal good" (NG 42).

Another line of criticism that has emerged against Foot argues for the superiority of evolutionary explanations over the kind of description that Foot relies on. In one such view, Foot's conception of function fails because she needs to draw on the notion of function as found in evolutionary biology. She must do this because the evolutionary view of function proves to be superior in its scope.[9] This criticism presumes that the evolutionary view, as the scientific account, is opposed to the Footian account, which tracks our everyday, armchair approach to the natural world. If something like the Footian notion of function is present in our everyday discourse, then, according to this view, we should revise everyday use to bring it into accord with evolutionary biology because its epistemological credentials are superior.[10]

This view is mistaken in its interpretation of Foot's theory in that Foot does not hope to displace the evolutionary view of function. Instead, she aims at a view of function that plays a separate theoretical role. Foot's naturalism is not the exclusive approach to evaluating organisms, though she does claim that is always in play when we make a judgment about an organism, because in any such judgment, we either assume or challenge the boundaries of a given species. In Foot's view, establishing what is normal for that species is an irreducibly interpretive task, and we are always employing some interpretation when we approach organisms, whether as armchair naturalists or evolutionary biologists. There are plenty of other ways of evaluating organisms, say, from the perspective of adaptive fitness, but the other evaluations depend upon natural normativity because they are evaluations of members of life forms.[11]

It is also important to recognize that Foot's view of function does not claim to explain the origin of species. It is not a biological theory in that sense; rather, it is a logical theory, a theory of the logic of statements about living things. Hence, the complaint that both Foot and Thompson fail to give us a "serious epistemological story about how we might come to know the truth of natural-historical judgments" is misplaced.[12] As Foot's goal is to show that a normative stance is essential to make claims about organisms, her concern is not about giving us an epistemological account of such claims and she can be satisfied with leaving the task to others.

Another criticism argues that Foot's ethics either yields repugnant results or it must appeal to a normative standard not grounded in natural norms.[13] Foot's ethical naturalism, in this view, would commit us to deeming disabled human beings to be defective. Given Foot's naturalistic framework, it is ad hoc to restrict ethical evaluation to an agent's rational will, or so it is claimed.[14] If Foot's view is indeed naturalistic, humans must be evaluated in just the same ways as other creatures, which would include defects of our physical integrity.

Contrary to this objection, Foot does not claim that natural norms apply only to the agent's rational will, and instead, she asserts that there are multiple dimensions of soundness that apply to human beings. In addition to physical soundness, we can also evaluate humans with regard to their wills. Foot's claim is that attributions of physical defect and moral defect have the same conceptual structure; this does not mean that they must have the same significance to us. Inasmuch as our moral defects are a product of choices that we have made, we are accountable for them. Our physical defects, however, are generally not the product of choices and this fact provides a rationale for divergent social attitudes toward moral and physical defects. It is also worth remembering that Foot insists that not every variation results in a defect. The same applies to human beings. While she cites certain physical conditions as defects, they are only so provided that they, in fact, impede humans from living a characteristically human life, and what counts as a characteristic human life is a matter of interpretation, not one of statistics. Hence, it would be rational to avoid correcting a "disability" that caused no genuine impediment to living a species-characteristic life. Foot could comfortably embrace the claims of the deaf community, for example, to realize distinctive human cultural goods.[15]

From nature to morality

I have defended Foot's ethical naturalism against criticisms that misinterpret what she means by "natural goodness" in the case of humans. It remains to ask whether the account achieves its goals when it is understood as Foot intended. Can Foot show morality to be something with a foundation in human nature, as she understands it? The account Foot gives is very promising, yet also programmatic. Foot believes that the moral virtues, together with prudence and virtues such as friendship and loyalty that pertain to human relationships, are justifiable on the basis of facts about human life. But which facts matter and why should they matter to us? If survival and reproduction are not the touchstone for human goodness, then what is? And why should we care about what is naturally good for humans?

In her view, there is more to being a good human than selecting correct and efficient means to whatever ends we set ourselves. There are some ends that we should take up. Foot believes that there is something it is to be good *qua* practically reasoning human that is independent of our actual aims and also of the historical contingencies of our various sorts of upbringing. In this respect, her views seem to contrast with those of John McDowell, who believes that the reasoning to which we should be responsive is defined by historically contingent factors.[16] For him, virtue is grounded in our upbringing, and its claim to being an objective moral outlook is the result of the fact that we submit the moral outlook imparted by our upbringing to ongoing scrutiny and reform. Foot, by contrast, argues for full-blooded objectivity and realism that includes determining the correct ends for us to pursue. Yet, one wonders, how can she be entitled to this strong sort of objectivity without appealing to the firm factual foundation of the biological notion of flourishing? Her argument seems to be that we are defective practical reasoners when we are not responsive to considerations that make human life go well wherever there is human life, and thus, she seems to deny that she is assuming some historically contingent standards of what it is to go well. If she renounces the idea that doing well is a bare biological given, how can she avoid McDowell's notion that our reasons stem from a conception of doing well that is a historically contingent construction?

Michael Thompson embraces a reading of Foot's intentions that seems to align her with McDowell's moral epistemology. He writes:

> [Foot] often seems to be justifying certain claims about human practical rationality where she might have emphasized the extent to which these thoughts are, on an account with this structure, self-validating. The human form of life is one in which considerations of justice, for example, characterize a sound practical reason. But this is not something we properly discover from a close study of human life. It must be given to us from inside, so to speak . . . That we operate with these thoughts is thus a *part* of what makes these thoughts true.[17]

I think that this is largely accurate, though a great deal depends on how we construe the phrase "*part* of" in the final sentence. It could suggest that we are free to refashion ourselves into what we would presently regard as immoral beings, but I do not think we need to read Foot in this way. Indeed, such a view would put Foot in uncomfortable company with the noncognitivist breakdown theories that she criticized earlier in her career, when she began advocating naturalism.

Yet, this dilemma—between a bare biological account of human nature, on the one hand, and an ethically informed, historically contingent account, on the other—is based on a false dichotomy. There is a third possibility—what it is to go well can be timelessly valid and universal, yet still dependent on our nature as rational animals. The idea is that there is a certain way that we must conceive ourselves if we are rational and certain reasons that must be genuine reasons for us, given how we necessarily conceive ourselves. This approach makes possible a sort of foundationalism grounded in what we must take ourselves to be if we are indeed self-conscious practical reasoners. Such an approach is not unprecedented as it is, after all, Immanuel Kant's approach. Practical reason itself imposes on us a certain way of thinking of our actions and ourselves such that, according to Kant, we must regard moral considerations as genuine and discount the force of considerations that oppose morality.

In the Kantian amendment to Foot's naturalism I am proposing, the core fact about human beings that supports her claims about morality is that we are agents—agency is a peculiar aspect of human beings in that it requires us to think of ourselves in a certain way; in particular, it requires us to think of ourselves as agents. This does not mean that we must have the occurrent thought "I am an agent" in order to possess agency, but we must be able to describe ourselves as engaging in some action, and to be able to do this, we must think of ourselves as members of a life form in which agency is normal. In *Intention*, Anscombe argues that for an action to be intentional, we must know what we are doing, without having to verify that we are doing it by observing that we are doing it. If I only know what I am doing from observation, a certain sense of the question "Why are you doing that?" is refused application, and I cannot be said to be acting intentionally under a certain description.[18] If someone calls attention to something that I did not realize I was doing, I will have to respond, "I did not realize I was doing that" and it is removed from candidacy as an intentional action, at least under that description. As pointed out earlier, to understand human actions likewise requires situating events against a background of norms for intentional actions. Hence, to understand human beings as agents requires, in this view, an understanding of the human form of life that incorporates norms for human action. These norms tell us what it is for a set of events to amount to an intentional action in a human. Thompson argues that even the most basic representations of oneself—for example, to have the thought that one is thinking— implicitly position oneself as a living thing engaged in a particular vital operation (i.e., thinking), and hence place oneself against the background of a form of life. For this reason, the concept of the human is, in Thompson's view, "the first life form concept." As he puts it, "the concept *human* is a pure concept of the understanding devoid of even the least empirical accretion."[19] Through one's own vital operations, then, one has nonobservational insight into one's own form of life. This second point underlines that our interpretation of our own form of life, unlike our relation to any other form of life, has a component not derived from any observable feature of the world. If Anscombe and Thompson are both correct, I simply must have such insight in order to describe myself as engaged in intentional action—I must have nonobservational insight into what I am doing under some description to be held to be acting intentionally under that description, and that action description implies a picture of the human life form in which a capacity for intentional action is normal.

What follows from this picture is that if I am capable of intentional action—if I am an agent—I must think of agency as a normal feature of the human life form. To describe oneself as acting, which is a prerequisite for being able to act, requires placing oneself against the background of a form of life in which such and such events result in performing an action. Hence, the capacity to act on reasons is a norm for anything that conceives of itself as acting, which is a prerequisite for being something that, in fact, acts. From this perspective, a human being lacking agency is, *ipso facto,* a defective human being.

Further, our necessary commitment to viewing agency as a norm commits us to viewing whatever damages our agency as, at least to that extent, bad. This includes actions, as actions that damage our agency are *pro tanto* bad actions. It is important to understand this as a norm for practical reason in human beings—it is part of what defines good practical reasoning in human beings. If we act, we cannot deny that agency is an aspect of human nature. In the context of the framework set out by Foot, where agency is an aspect of our form of life, agency is not morally neutral because one who lacks it is defective *qua* human. And it is a feature of our nature that must register with us in our norms for action because we must cast ourselves against the background of this norm in order to act. Norms of practical reason that would allow us to wantonly damage agency for the sake of some transient desire would pit us against this picture of ourselves. The inevitable centrality of agency to our self-conception supports a virtue I will term "proto-justice," in order to underline that it is not a fleshed-out conception of justice.

My claim is that we are defective human beings if we fail to exhibit protojustice because we are thereby defective in our agency.

A question that remains here is—"Why should I care whether or not I am defective as a human being?" Part of the force of this objection comes from our tendency to understand the category "human" only from the standpoint of the natural sciences. The force of the argument for the foundational importance of agency in a neoAristotelian account depends on hearing the concept "human" on a different register, as a concept that we employ whenever we think of ourselves or other human beings. In such cases, the concept "human" is playing the role of picking out the life form of which we are members; it is the logical apparatus that I must use to describe myself if I am a self-conscious agent. This makes being a defective human quite a different matter from recognizing that the roots on a plant are good. Whether I care about the latter depends on my interests, as I can legitimately acknowledge that pouring this solution on the plant will make its roots whither, and I can do that rationally, especially if it is a weed plant threatening my food crop. Why can I not acknowledge that sticking a knife into someone will harm him and still rationally do that? Of course, I can, when it is a case of someone who is posing a threat to others or me. Yet, I cannot, I claim, when it is done merely with the intention of getting his wallet. The failure to properly value human agency involved in killing for gain goes against reasons that are implicit in every description I make of others and myself as acting. If agency is essential to being a nondefective human, then we cannot act well in compromising our agency for the sake of inessential goods. Nothing can be a justifiable norm for human practical reason that is pitted against an essential feature of our natural goodness.

In this account, then, what is wrong with the egoist who recognizes only the fulfillment of his own interests as valuable? The egoist is irrational in that he sets aims and acts on his own desires and interests, perhaps with a view to maximizing their fulfillment. When, in enacting his plans, he describes himself as acting, he implicitly appeals to a norm for human beings that he contradicts in his reasoning about how to act. His reasoning is defective inasmuch as he fails to acknowledge the value of human agency that he implicitly appeals to in his description of himself as acting; in framing these pursuits, he describes them in terms that advert to the objective goodness of human agency. One might think he can value his own agency while discounting the value of the agency of others. Yet, if he acknowledges the goodness of his own agency because it is a natural standard, and not just because it aligns with his interests to do so, then he cannot deny that this standard is a natural standard for all other beings of his kind. And he cannot maintain that, in the same objective terms, there is a standard for human beings that allows us to dispense with the agency of others whenever it conflicts with our desires and interests. Also, the egoist cannot claim that this goodness is not relevant to his pursuits because it does not matter whether he takes an interest in them; the reasons that being good as a human being generates do not depend on his desires. If he does not recognize the reasons, then he is defective in his reasoning. I am making the claim that we cannot understand ourselves as agents without understanding the requirements of protojustice, at least when we have certain rudimentary facts about human vulnerability to depredation on hand. He can adopt a principle of acknowledging only the value of his own interests, but the principle is arbitrary, grounded on mere subjective whim. If this account is correct, the egoist renounces the reasoned basis for joint human endeavors because he does not acknowledge what is objectively valuable. Yet, the irrational agent does not necessarily fall into misery; he simply fails to live as reason recommends, and that may or may not have grave consequences for him or others.

There is a possible maneuver on the part of the clever egoist—one that would consist of an attempt to define oneself as a member of a distinctive form of life—but I think that, short of actually possessing a truly distinctive physiology, this claim cannot hold up. For example, being invulnerable to blows or stabbing, or being able to photosynthesize, would be differences of the sort that would render certain of norms of our form of life irrelevant. Whether I care about being a defective human does not depend on my having plans that involve being a nondefective human; it depends only on my being an agent. Being an agent requires me to understand myself in relation to my life form, and this understanding has normative implications.

My claim then is that human agency is a crucial aspect of human nature for providing the sort of timelessly valid foundation for virtues that Foot was seeking. Any rationality-conferring second nature will also confer agency. Rationality and agency go hand in hand for just the reason that McDowell gives in "Two Sorts of Naturalism." As he puts it:

> . . . something whose physical make-up left no free play in how it manifested itself in interactions with the rest of reality, or something whose physical make-up, although it left such free play, somehow precluded the development of the imagination required to contemplate alternatives, could not acquire reason. (1998: 171)

The acquisition of reason goes hand in hand with the acquisition of agency. Yet, the conceptual structure of agency is such that it forces us to think of it as a norm for organisms of the sort that we are, or so I have argued. According to this argument, then, we must think of ourselves as falling under certain very general requirements if we acquire reason. Human nature therefore has its own normative foundations, and these may indeed be foundations for moral virtues, just as Foot posited. Yet, she rightly worried about a further challenge to her views to be found in the works of Friedrich Nietzsche, and it is to that challenge that I turn in the next chapter.

CHAPTER SEVEN

Nietzsche and morality

"How is it, one may ask, that philosophers today do not even try to refute Nietzsche, and seem to feel morality as firm as ever under their feet? Why do we not argue with him as we argue with other philosophers of the past? Part of the answer seems to be that a confrontation with Nietzsche is a difficult thing to arrange." (VV 82)

Throughout her career, Foot argued against immoralism, by which she means the view that there is at least equally good reason to be immoral as there is to be moral. The most important forms of this view, for her, are to be found in Plato's presentation of the ancient Sophists and in the writings of Friedrich Nietzsche, to whom she devoted two articles and the final chapter of *Natural Goodness*. Immoralism is important to confront, she believes, because immoralists are not just a figment of the philosopher's imagination; they actually exist. She believes that Adolf Hitler provides a historical example of an immoralist. Although Hitler no doubt thought that he was attempting to do something good, he was willing to commit atrocities while entirely ignoring the injustice of his actions and commands for the sake of achieving what he thought to be good. In his view, there are goods to be achieved that justify violating the norms of justice. Those committed to morality hold that we should not violate norms of justice even for the sake of genuine goods. Foot believes that she finds views reminiscent of Hitler's dismissive attitude to justice expressed in Nietzsche. While she denies the idea that Hitler directly embodies Nietzsche's ideals, she endorses Thomas Mann's view that Nietzsche seems naïvely romantic after Hitler (NG 114).[1] So, Foot thinks Nietzsche's philosophy and immoralism, in general, are worth taking very seriously in philosophy. Yet, in the end, she considers Nietzsche to be a dangerous influence, and immoralism a mistaken philosophical position.

In this chapter, I will examine Foot's criticisms of Nietzsche. I argue that although she attempts to take Nietzsche seriously, Foot's criticisms in some instances miss their mark. When properly understood, Nietzsche's views often complement Foot's philosophical position, especially inasmuch as she gives a prominent place in her view of the human good to considerations of self-interest, independently of considerations of morality. In other respects, Nietzsche's views pose challenges to Foot's claims for morality. I conclude that although Foot succeeds in defending an objective conception of human excellence, Nietzsche provides compelling reasons to doubt our ability to ground the virtues as they have been traditionally conceived on that conception. In the view I will argue for here, Foot ought to admit, with Nietzsche, that her views on human excellence provide grounds for the revision of traditional morality.

Is Nietzsche an immoralist?

Foot believes that Nietzsche deserves the appellation "immoralist," though this may be in part because Nietzsche calls himself an immoralist.[2] Yet, we must be clear about what this term means for Nietzsche, and whether it matches the meaning that Foot gives to it.

As discussed in Chapter 2, Foot holds that the concept of morality has some determinate content; a rule requiring us to clap our hands three times in an hour cannot be part of a moral code, at least not without a special background connecting that activity to human well-being. Foot states that there are "definitional criteria" of moral good and evil, which belong to the concept of morality itself, and from which it follows that Hitler's treatment of Jews was morally indefensible (MD 7). Foot apparently holds that Nietzsche's immoralism extends to the denial of morality even in this spare, definitional sense. She writes of Nietzsche that he was "prepared to throw out rules of justice in the interests of producing a stronger and more splendid type of man" (VV 92). If she is correct, Nietzsche would be a stark immoralist with a genuine kinship to Hitler in his willingness to violate rights for the sake of a "higher" purpose, despite disagreeing with Hitler over the purpose aimed at.

Yet, whether Nietzsche fits such stark immoralism is quite contestable. After all, as he states:

> It goes without saying that I do not deny – unless I am a fool – that many actions called immoral ought to be avoided and resisted, or that many called moral ought to be done and encouraged – but I think the one should be encouraged and the other avoided *for other reasons than hitherto*. We have to *learn to think differently* – in order at last, perhaps very late on, to attain even more: *to feel differently*.[3]

This passage suggests that Nietzsche's immoralism is rather sophisticated in that it is based on a sort of moral concern. His concern seems to be that thinking and feeling in moral terms is harmful to us, and that without acting in some of the ways that morality prohibits, or giving up acting in some of the ways that morality enjoins, we can avoid those harmful effects. There are two central claims here—first, there is a way of thinking and feeling that is characteristic of morality, and second, these manners of thinking and feeling are harmful. If these claims are true, then clearly, one committed to moral ends such as promoting human well-being would want to take them seriously. Foot recognizes this; as she puts it, "insofar as Nietzsche is suggesting that morality in general and Christian morality in particular has [harmful effects,] he is at least arguing on moral grounds" (VV 93). It appears then that Foot takes Nietzsche to be arguing on moral grounds for overcoming morality. Yet, as I will argue, it is not a complete overcoming of morality, but only overcoming a specific version of morality. There is a further claim that Nietzsche subscribes to—the premises of morality are false, just as the premises of alchemy are false.[4] Before exploring the first two claims, let us focus on this third claim.

Of all Nietzsche's claims about morality, the claim that the premises of morality are false is the least straightforward to interpret. As Foot asks concerning this claim, "Does [morality] then have premises? What could these be?" (NG 99). Of course, the answer depends on what is meant by morality, as the term has wider and narrower senses that both Foot and Nietzsche move between, often without observing that they are doing so. In the wider sense, which corresponds to Foot's definitional criteria, any standard of conduct that takes account of human well-being will count as morality.[5] In the narrower sense, morality refers to a particular code of conduct that meets the definitional criteria. As Foot herself notes, somewhat inconsistently with her characterization of Nietzsche as an immoralist, Nietzsche's views appear to have much in common with Greek morality (VV 92). This characterization of Nietzsche is inconsistent because Foot takes him to be contesting "morality in general" and advocating for a replacement of moral value with "quasi-aesthetic" values (VV 92). Yet, it appears that Nietzsche is not contesting morality in the wide sense, but only morality as it has been understood in Christendom—an understanding of morality that arguably continues to exert a considerable influence on those who have abandoned the faith. To the extent that Nietzsche advocates quasiaesthetic values, he is not advocating replacing morality in the wider sense, since when he advocates such values, he does so on the basis of their being, in some sense, better for us than the values we currently embrace.[6]

What then are the premises of Western morality that Nietzsche holds to be false, and what are the consequences of rejecting them? The premises he has in mind may be given as follows:

1   There are categorically binding and universal quasi-legal prohibitions and obligations (moral requirements).
2   Moral requirements serve the greater good.
3   Moral requirements override other requirements.

These aspects of Western morality are obviously derived from its Christian origins; the decrees of God, conceived as an omniscient and benevolent legislator, would surely have exactly these features. Yet, morality in this sense has outlived our ability to take its foundations for granted, and these premises are part of the background against which much modern moral philosophy has operated even when it does not assume the existence of God. Immanuel Kant and modern British moral philosophers took up the task of vindicating morality so conceived, without depending on the existence of God. Nietzsche thinks all of these premises are false and contests them. Similarly, Foot contests (2) understood in a utilitarian sense, (3), and the version of (1) that she stands on is highly qualified relative to the tradition. Hence, as should be evident by the end of this chapter, Foot's views closely parallel those of Nietzsche in many respects.

Nietzsche believes these premises of Western morality are intimately tied to a belief in God and, in turn, collapse when that belief is taken away. Essentially, the premises of Western morality propose a "law conception of ethics," as Anscombe termed it.[7] Without a lawmaker, this conception becomes incoherent, or so Nietzsche thinks. He contests (2) with his historical account of morality as well as his psychological analysis of guilt. According to Nietzsche's historical account, morality was certainly not devised to serve the greater good; instead, it is the product of a cultural revolution in the ancient world. The so-call "slave revolt" was an inversion of values held by masters, who, naturally enough, valued themselves. As Nietzsche describes in the First Treatise of *On the Genealogy of Morality,* "good" was used by nobles in reference to themselves, in contrast with all things base, common, and vulgar.[8] What these aristocrats labeled "good" did not have anything to do with usefulness, which would count among the qualities of tools and slaves, and mark a lack of nobility. Yet, the slave revolt in morality inverted these values, so that it was "good" to be of use to others, and the idle, leisurely smugness of the master was "evil."

One might think that this inversion of noble values would result in a morality of which (2) is true, and yet, despite lauding usefulness to others, slave morality has psychological effects that render it harmful to those who adopt it. It demands that we restrain drives that would otherwise receive free expression; the occasional, inevitable venting of those drives or even the inner experience of them results in repercussions of bad conscience. The result is a struggle to obtain good conscience, that is, to live up to the dictates of a morality that is fundamentally a matter of turning against our own nature. As Nietzsche writes:

> All instincts that do not discharge outwardly *turn themselves inwards* – this is what I call the *internalizing* of man . . . Hostility, cruelty, pleasure in persecution, in assault, in change, in destruction – all of that turning itself against the possessors of such instincts: *that* is the origin of "bad conscience."[9]

The self-denial that internalization entails was essential to the inversion of values at the origin of Western morality, according to Nietzsche. By demonstrating psychological power over their drives, the priestly proponents of slave morality could uphold themselves as superior to those who permit themselves direct satisfaction of their desires; they possess a power more subtle and refined than brute strength. For Nietzsche, the motives behind the "selflessness" of slave morality are but another way of asserting power and reclaiming the right to create values. So, the claim that morality serves the greater good reflects a view that proponents of slave morality have regarding their own moral values, but it is a false view, as it ignores the psychological costs of internalization.

The claim that moral values override all others is also an essential component of this moral system, inasmuch as it aims at mastering powerful drives that are seeking an outlet. Thus, those who have internalized slave morality find moral judgments to have an overriding force, but that does not mean that they should have such force. Since the results of internalization are weakening and self-hatred, whatever good morality has done must be weighed with these psychological effects in mind. If another path to attaining the desired ends of morality without such self-laceration truly exists, then surely we should seek it, and this seems to be precisely what Nietzsche has in mind when calling for an investigation into the "value of our values."

Charity and compassion

A central claim in Nietzsche's critique of morality is that the ways of thinking and feeling that characterize compassion are especially harmful to us. This is a significant challenge to Foot's program in moral philosophy because compassion would seem to be a necessary for someone to possess the virtue of benevolence, or "charity" in Foot's terms.[10] If compassion is harmful to those who experience it as well as to its target, as Nietzsche claims, then there is a significant problem for the status of benevolence as a virtue, and so, Nietzsche's view poses a direct challenge to one of Foot's central commitments.

One component of Nietzsche's critique of compassion is a challenge to how we think of compassion. Nietzsche believes that we idealize compassion and deceive ourselves concerning our motives when we act out of compassion. Indeed, Nietzsche holds that the capacity to understand another empathically essentially involves "rapid dissimulation" of our motives.[11] If we examine our motives in helping others, we find something like this:

> An accident which happens to another offends us: it would make us aware of our impotence, and perhaps of our cowardice, if we did not go to assist him. Or it brings with it in itself a diminution of our honor in the eyes of others or in our own eyes. Or an accident and suffering incurred by another constitutes a signpost to some danger to us; and it can have a painful effect upon us simply as a token of human vulnerability and fragility in general. We repel this kind of pain and offence and requite it through an act of compassion; it may contain subtle self-defense or even a piece of revenge.[12]

An act of compassion is self-defense inasmuch as through it, we witness our own power over the vulnerability that plagues the sufferer. It is revenge inasmuch as through it, I demonstrate my power over the other who requires my help; through my compassionate act, I demonstrate superiority over the recipient of my compassion, who was perhaps my superior in the past.

Could these features be merely accidental features of compassion that we could avoid and thereby attain true compassion? Nietzsche appears to think that we cannot. These features are not qualities of a degenerate form of compassion but, according to him, they are essential features of compassion. He wants us to see that compassion is not necessarily what those who value it conceive it to be. Descriptive psychology can displace idealizations of ourselves that serve our psychological needs, and this may be beneficial as our idealizations may be maladaptive. Nietzsche believes that this is the case with our conception of compassion—we have an idealized picture of compassion, and we are motivated to defend that idealization because the feeling of pleasure that results from acting compassionately stems from seeing ourselves in light of that idealized picture. Through honest observation of our own emotional and cognitive processes, Nietzsche hopes to show that we are short-sighted in holding onto this idealization of compassion, even if we get pleasure from acting in light of it. Nietzsche applies a kind of naturalistic, functionalist analysis to that vocabulary that he believes debunks many of our views about ourselves. Of course, he pursues this method in a rather armchair manner that does not yield serviceable scientific knowledge by today's standards. Consequently, the most we can say about these observations without further confirmation is that they have the air of plausibility. Still, even if Nietzsche's descriptive claims are sustained by psychological investigation, this fact need not discredit compassion altogether.[13] After all, compassion, so understood, still generates acts of benevolence, even if the motives of the compassionate person are not directly targeted at the welfare of others.

What is so shortsighted about compassion that we should give it up in spite of the pleasures that we derive from acting in accordance with it? Here, Nietzsche takes a second line of argument against compassion, which consists of a critical examination of compassion in its ideal form, according to which the compassionate individual takes the suffering of another as though it were his own. This ideal would lead, according to Nietzsche, to an increase in suffering. He states, "Supposing it was dominant even for a single day, mankind would immediately perish of it."[14] This is because taking compassion as a principle of action would mean that "we would have to suffer from our own ego and at the same time from the ego of the other, and would thus voluntarily encumber ourselves with a double load of irrationality instead of making the burden of our own as light as possible."[15] Nietzsche's assumption here is that even if we developed perfect compassion and acted accordingly, we would by no means eliminate suffering, and we would thereby suffer from the inevitable suffering of others. Nietzsche thereby argues that even by a utilitarian standard, it would not be rational to seek to cultivate compassion.

But of course, Nietzsche does not accept that standard, and so this argument is not the basis on which he rejects compassion as a harmful ideal. Rather, the central reason Nietzsche rejects compassion as an ideal is that it implies that human life ought to be directed at the mitigation of pain, which Nietzsche believes should only be a peripheral aspect of our lives. In contrast with Jeremy Bentham, who claimed that pleasure and pain are our "sovereign masters," Nietzsche believes that pleasure and pain are "incidental states and trivialities."[16] To set the abolition of suffering as an end is to aim at something that would make human beings ridiculous, as we would be aiming at nothing more than being comfortable. It

would make for a "religion of snug coziness."[17] The harm we do
ourselves in embracing such an ideal consists not only of lowering
our sights, but also denying the conditions of human growth,
which include significant suffering. As Nietzsche states, "they want
to *help* and have no thought that there is a personal necessity of
misfortune; that terrors, deprivations, impoverishments, midnights,
adventures, risks, and blunders are as necessary for me and you as
their opposites."[18] And again, he states, "The Discipline of suffering,
of *great* suffering – don't you know that *this* discipline has been the
sole cause of every enhancement in humanity so far?"[19]

Nietzsche's overall teaching on compassion, then, seems to be
this—if we look at compassion as it actually operates, it serves
specific personal, psychological needs, and is much less purely
in the service of others than its advocates would have us believe.
Ignoring the facts of descriptive psychology, these advocates
attempt to promote an ideal of human life that would make us
into something despicably shortsighted, and with decidedly limited
aims. Compassion in this form is therefore nothing to be esteemed.
Note that this is not to say that we ought to merely let others suffer;
Nietzsche seems to take for granted that when confronted with
suffering, we *will* generally help.[20] But such reflexive helping is not
necessarily to be lauded. Instead of compassion (*Mitleid*, literally:
"suffering-with"), he encourages us to seek shared joy (*Mitfreude*).
Presumably, by this, he means joy at the attainment of difficult
things that require discipline and suffering rather than complacent
enjoyment of the snug coziness he derides.

To all of this, Foot replies that although compassion may
sometimes be a sham, "thinking of the ordinary unpretentious men
and women who seem to find special happiness in working for the
relief of suffering, one must surely find Nietzsche's dismissive views
on compassion rather silly" (NG 107). Further, she claims:

> . . . love and other forms of kindness are needed by every one of
> us when misfortune strikes, and may be a sign of strength rather
> than weakness in those who are sorry for us. We may reasonably
> think, moreover, that charity makes for happiness in the one who
> has it, as hardness does not. (NG 108)

Foot is surely correct in claiming that acts of charity would be
needful even if there were no truly charitable actions as measured by

the motives of those who pursue them. Yet, I think Foot's response to the descriptive psychological aspect of Nietzsche's critique of compassion is somewhat miscalculated. His views on compassion are not dismissive, but detailed and nuanced, and, far from being "silly," they raise interesting questions, even if they turn out to be false.[21] Let us assume, for the sake of argument, that Nietzsche is correct in his descriptive psychology of compassion. This does not mean that there will be no compassionate acts, but only that such acts will be done from different, nonaltruistic motives. It does not appear that Nietzsche himself believes this descriptive psychology utterly undermines the value of compassion. Rather, his aim is to refute an idealization of compassion held by those who believe it to be essential to morality, as we find in Schopenhauer and some utilitarians. Getting this idealization out of the way allows Nietzsche to ask whether compassion best meets our needs, whether the needs are those of one who experiences compassion or the target of compassion. There is no need to hold on to the idealized picture of compassion in order to value compassion. Rather, if Nietzsche's claims are true, we can calibrate our conception of charity to the facts of our actual motives. If compassionate individuals are actually alleviating a sense of their own vulnerability or impotence, this fact need not detract from the value of compassion; Nietzsche's critique is rhetorically calculated to strike hard at those who come to his text with an idealized vision of compassionate persons, but once we extract the message of his critique from that rhetoric, we find claims that are neither surprising nor overly cynical. They fall far short of La Rochefoucauld's claim that "virtue is (most often) vice disguised."[22] That is because Nietzsche is not claiming that to meet those needs is vicious; it is not bad to meet those needs, and if there is dissimulation involved, it is clearly not deliberate. These are points that Foot can adopt.

Now, let us examine charity as an ideal—does Foot's response meet Nietzsche's challenge to compassion as an ideal as it is found in charitable acts? It does, but only partially, and it fails to benefit from the insights that could come from taking a somewhat less defensive posture toward that challenge. We must constantly remind ourselves of Nietzsche's targets, which include Schopenhauer and the classical utilitarians. Foot should take Nietzsche's side against these targets; after all, she does not believe that charity is the only virtue or the supreme virtue, and she allows for the independent reason-giving force of considerations such as self-interest and desire-fulfillment.[23] In other words, she thinks that such considerations may sometimes trump moral considerations. Nietzsche agrees, but moreover, he is ready to undertake a revaluation of moral values as an outgrowth of the project of de-fictionalizing morality by allowing that we act in accordance with self-interest more often than we think. Schopenhauer and the classical utilitarians inherit the legacy of the Judeo-Christian tradition, and their central values reflect it, according to Nietzsche. The centrality of eliminating pain that is found in their views reflects weariness with life because pain and suffering are ever-present features of human life, even when it goes well. Pain can be shrugged off by more vigorous people, and thus, the elimination of pain is not an overarching goal for them. Nietzsche is challenging us to think about our ultimate goals, and doing so in a way that is as direct and explicit as in Foot's writings.

As for Foot's remark that charity makes for happiness in a way that hardness does not, I think, here again, we find a straw man of Nietzsche's actual position. He is not advocating hardness, but rather a more balanced approach to compassion and charity than can be found in the writings of his immediate predecessors and contemporaries. He is encouraging us to recognize the role of pain and suffering in human growth. As any parent knows, a certain amount of pain and suffering is an inevitable part of growing up; one could imagine sheltering a child from this reality of human life, as did Siddhartha Gautama's parents according to Buddhist legend, but surely this would prevent or at least delay psychological growth. Hence, our charity must be calibrated to broader concerns about human growth and development, and this is surely Nietzsche's point. To be good parents, a little hardness may be necessary. That means resisting a temptation to resolve difficult conflicts for one's children, to hide the darker aspects of life from them, or to suppress their mildly risky activities. Hence, Foot's point that charity is needful is correct and not contradicted by Nietzsche; still, the charity we need is not that which we find advocated in Schopenhauer and utilitarianism.

Justice and the higher man

In her first treatment of Nietzsche, Foot complains that he is willing to admit that unjust acts might be morally permissible if they are done for the sake of a greater good. This is a key part of her charge that he is an immoralist. In *Natural Goodness*, this same charge is included within a more general claim—that Nietzsche denies the existence of types of action that are intrinsically wrong. Foot finds this denial where Nietzsche writes:

> To talk of justice and injustice *in themselves* is devoid of all sense; in itself injuring, doing violence, pillaging, destroying naturally cannot be "unjust," insofar as life acts *essentially* – that is, in its basic functions – in an injuring, violating, pillaging, destroying manner and cannot be *thought* at all without this character.[24]

Foot takes this remark to be saying that some injurious, destructive acts are permissible, or at least, not unjust, because they are simply a part of life. She dismisses this argument because she takes it to involve "illicit identification of features of the plant and animal worlds with *human acts* of injury or oppression" (NG 110). Whereas plants and nonhuman animals may act in ways that are injurious to other life, we cannot hold such life forms accountable because they lack rational agency. We cannot adopt a sweeping permission to act injuriously on the basis of the fact that some, or even all, non-human life forms injure others. She finds somewhat more compelling another argument he makes for the denial of intrinsically unjust kinds of actions. According to this argument, we cannot deem actions right or wrong without taking into account the nature of the person who has performed them. As textual support for attributing this position to Nietzsche, she cites a passage in which he describes warriors engaged in murder and rape as "pranksome," as well as a passage from *Thus Spoke Zarathustra* that appears to assert that there are no universal rights or wrongs.[25]

It is unclear whether Foot reads Nietzsche correctly in any of these passages. In the first passage, Nietzsche is clearly denying that justice and injustice exist as natural categories. Of course, Foot disagrees with this, but only in view of an innovative conception of living things and of how the human will can be evaluated in a manner that is identical in its logical structure to evaluations of other forms of life.[26] In the absence of such a notion, it no doubt seems sensible to deny that justice and injustice exist as natural categories, but that does not necessarily mean that Nietzsche sees just any legal code as justifiable, whatever its commands or prohibitions.[27] In other words, the passage need not be read as trying to extract permission for injurious actions by appeal to the conditions necessary for life. He is simply denying that specific norms of justice are somehow prescribed by nature.

Concerning the second passage, Nietzsche is describing how the acts were viewed by their perpetrators, and is not endorsing or trivializing the acts by calling them "pranksome." Indeed, he says that these barbaric nobles exhibit an "appalling light-heartedness."[28]

In the third passage, from *Zarathustra*, Nietzsche's protagonist lauds the overthrow of the "mole and dwarf who says: 'Good for all, evil for all."[29] Remarkably, Foot does not appear to notice that Nietzsche is here using the terms "good and *evil*," rather than "good and bad." It is evident that this is part of Nietzsche's railing against Judeo-Christian morality or slave morality, which lays down its norms in a quasilegal form of universal imperatives and prohibitions. There is no need to read Nietzsche as denying that there are some actions and traits, specified with suitable generality, that are good or bad. Obviously, it is not enough to make one an immoralist of the sort that Foot targets to deny that there are universal prescriptions and prohibitions. Given that there seems to be insufficient evidence for attributing to Nietzsche the view that murder might be allowable when done by the right sort of person, Foot's worries seem ungrounded.

Again, Foot's worries about Nietzsche's immoralism seem to prevent her from registering the significance of his concerns about justice. These concerns are summarized in the passage in which Foot finds Nietzsche denying intrinsically just or unjust acts. Nietzsche writes:

> A legal system conceived of as sovereign and universal, not as a means in the battle of power complexes, but rather as means *against* all battle generally . . . would be a principle *hostile to life*, a destroyer and dissolver of man, an attempt to kill the future of man, a sign of weariness, a secret pathway to nothingness.[30]

Here, Nietzsche is diagnosing motives for adhering to an ideal of perfect justice as a drive to overcome struggle, which he views as essential to life. Whatever one may think of Nietzsche's point here, one can take this as against justice *tout court* only if one holds an extreme, uncompromising idea of that virtue. It is open to Foot to take a position exactly parallel to that which I suggested in relation to Nietzsche's critique of compassion. That is, she can deny that we need to hold such an uncompromising conception of justice.

Surely, there is something to be said for Nietzsche's position here. Justice as it is and is ever likely to be will surely take place in a complex web of power relations, and to wish to overcome that fact is empty and futile. To calibrate our notion of justice to fit the facts of human life might mean, among other things, giving greater weight to the virtue of mercy in our approach to punishment. We find again, in short, that Nietzsche is far less toxic than Foot takes him to be, and again, his insights may contribute to a richer understanding of virtue.

Morality without illusions

Foot leaves us with a very grim picture of Nietzsche. She writes:

> . . . those who take his attack on morality simply as a rather edifying call to authenticity and self-fulfillment are deluding themselves; the proof of this lying precisely in what he said about there being no right or wrong actions considered in themselves. (NG 114)

According to Foot, Nietzsche missteps through becoming so engrossed in a Romantic ideal of genius that he loses touch with basic facts of human life. Thus, she finds it necessary to assert, against him, that our form of life depends on norms such that "if, for instance, a stranger should come on us when we are sleeping he will not think it all right to kill us or appropriate the tools that we need for the next day's work" (NG 114). However, if there is anyone who needs to hear this, it is not Nietzsche. Far from being out of touch with the facts of human life, he is arguably more in touch with such facts than most moral philosophers. Further, he is in touch with the context of his utterance in a way that is lost on some of his readers. For, while Foot is concerned with justifying morality in the widest possible context, Nietzsche is worried about addressing a culture in which morality is widely accepted, taught, and, too often, unquestioned. In that context, Nietzsche highlights the cruelty that is wrought in the name of bringing about the internalization of moral norms, and the ongoing psychological struggle we face with bad conscience. He is hopeful that by getting beyond good and evil, we can move beyond the struggle to attain a "merely good conscience," which is an uninspiring goal, even if it does prove difficult to attain. Of course, in the light of spectacular scandals and atrocities, one could wonder if this message still has relevance. No doubt our view is distorted by the fact that criminality and atrocities are broadcast to us at every possible hour, whereas the struggles of the majority of people with their consciences and our ever more anxious attempts to instill morality in the next generation go mostly unnoticed.

Foot seems not to notice Nietzsche's central concern with the cruelty wrought in the name of morality itself, and writes:

> Human life, unlike the life of animals, is lived according to norms that are known and taken as patterns by those whose norms they are. So we have to teach children what they may and may not do. Nor could these norms be taught simply by telling children that they are to be courageous and 'authentic,' however important it is to encourage them to be daring and also to allow them to discover their true desires. (NG 114)

It is troubling to hear this coming from someone who has called us to take Nietzsche seriously. Clearly, Nietzsche was not merely calling us to be authentic, but calling for a searching, rational inquiry into morality. While Foot takes herself to be attending to the facts of human life in saying that children need to be taught what they may and may not do, Nietzsche is calling us to look at the psychological effects of our teaching and see whether it truly advances the ends we are hoping to attain. That is how we are supposed to look for the "value of our values." Of course, Nietzsche did inveigh against the "morality of custom," but not in order to support an anarchic moral free-for-all; rather, if considered in very broad strokes, he can be read as a continuation of the program Immanuel Kant called for in "What is Enlightenment?" where he asks us to dare to question our inherited moral norms and thereby emerge from a period of cultural immaturity. The idea is to arrive at better norms for conduct, not to do away with all norms.

In light of some views that she shares with Nietzsche, Foot seems overly confident that the foundations she lays out in *Natural Goodness* will confirm traditional moral values. As she puts it in the

"Postscript" to that work, echoing Wittgenstein, "in a way, nothing is settled, but everything is left as it was" (NG 116). Yet, this is not necessarily the case. Given that she is leaving room for independent reason-giving force on the part of our interests and desires, over and against moral considerations, our inherited morality, or at least the idealized image of that morality, may not stand untouched by her framework. It also is not clear how we are supposed to go from a general picture of the good human to the moral codes we are supposed to be teaching our children. Presumably, this would take place against the background of a detailed psychological picture of human beings. We find the beginnings of such a picture in Nietzsche, who also points out that we will need to question our values "from the most diverse perspectives."[31] For him, this included all scientific inquiry, including physiology and psychology. Foot seems ready to wash her hands off these issues in saying that these are matters "in which philosophy can claim no special voice" and that, no doubt, is true, but just because philosophy cannot claim exclusive dominion over a subject does not mean that philosophers can ignore it (NG 108).

Foot was drawn to write about Nietzsche through both an aversion to some of his conclusions as well as through her affinity with him in her readiness to question received teachings about morality, such as the overridingness of moral considerations. In other ways, she overlooks their shared views. Part of the impetus for turning to virtue as an important concept for moral philosophy was precisely in marking out the territory for meaningful moral philosophy in the absence of religiously sanctioned moral laws. Her project leaves us with a notion of human excellence that encompasses prudence as well as justice, charity, mercy, and other virtues. This shift is not merely a conceptual one. We face the task of re-inventing justice and charity in light of taking our individual interests and desires more seriously than Christian morality previously sanctioned. Contrary to Foot, Nietzsche's views make a significant contribution to the advancement of this worthwhile project.

CHAPTER EIGHT

Philippa Foot's moral vision

"I have been asked the very pertinent question as to where all this leaves disputes about substantial moral questions. Do I really believe that I have described a method for settling them all? The proper reply is that in a way nothing is settled, but everything is left as it was." (NG 116)

In saying that *Natural Goodness* leaves everything as it was, Foot is paraphrasing Wittgenstein, who said of philosophy in general that it "leaves everything as it is."[1] Foot seems to have conceived of her work as serving to clear away confusions about how we operate using our moral concepts. As she puts it, her goal is "to get rid of some intruding philosophical theories and abstractions that tend to trip us up" (NG 116). In "Goodness and Choice," she claims that her opponents are "in the grip of a theory" (VV 145). Again, she echoes Wittgenstein, who says that he was held "captive by a picture" while writing the *Tractatus Logico-Philosophicus.*[2] Foot's echoes of Wittgenstein reflect a consistent metaphilosophical view that she holds throughout most of her career—a view which is owed to her reading of Wittgenstein's *Philosophical Investigations.* The *Investigations* contain a series of reflections on the proper task of philosophy, as well as a diagnosis of how philosophy can go astray. According to Wittgenstein, philosophy, when done properly, puts us in contact with our language in all of its complexity and nuance;

but when it goes wrong, philosophy imposes artificial requirements for clarity and simplicity in the employment of our concepts, and seduces us into adopting artificial theories regarding what we mean by our concepts. Foot surely takes the view that Hare and other noncognitivists offered a philosophical view in the latter, bad sense, and may have thought that utilitarianism was another such view.

The rhetoric of this metaphilosophical view is dangerous, however; it is easy to be unfair to opponents by characterizing them as "in the grip of a theory." Another problem with metaphilosophical Wittgensteinianism of this sort is that it may belie the role of philosophical reflection in social reform. Utilitarians have clearly been involved in social reform, from highlighting the backwardness of common law in the United Kingdom, where it originated in the eighteenth century, to decrying animal cruelty in agriculture in the late twentieth century. Wittgensteinians may want to say that the philosopher is not speaking as a philosopher in advocating for social change, but I see no reason to agree with this view.

My worry is that Foot's adherence to these Wittgensteinian dicta leads her to not only feign neutrality within her own work, but also to dismiss a plausible reading of her work as engaged in a sort of critical social theory. In representing her work as a morally neutral, conceptual project of uprooting "intruding" philosophical theories, Foot appears vulnerable to the same criticisms Murdoch raises against Hare in "Vision and Choice in Morality" (discussed in Chapter 1). As we have seen, Foot has substantial moral disagreements with consequentialists of all stripes, but part of her disagreement with them stems from a conceptual matter— whether we can meaningfully speak of "good states of affairs." Clearly, it is a legitimate philosophical project to question the conceptual foundations of a moral view. Yet, the extent to which her arguments on this issue are taken as definitive may turn on whether her audience shares her substantive moral commitments, as well as implicit views on other matters. A strong point of Murdoch's paper was to recognize that moral philosophers, when presenting themselves as working on a delimited set of issues in moral philosophy, are in fact always relying on background beliefs about the world that are, themselves, contestable. So, Murdoch diagnosed Hare's moral philosophy as relying on a conception of the world according to which, we are all in "the same empirical and rationally comprehensible world," and she contrasts this with a picture according to which, "we live in a world whose mystery transcends us and that morality is the exploration of that mystery in so far as it concerns each individual."[3]

Clearly, Foot's vision is not the one that Murdoch attributes to Hare, the Liberal Protestant vision in which freedom is of paramount value. But her views do not align with the Catholic, Marxist, or existentialist camps that Murdoch sees as major alternative moral visions. Though Foot identifies herself as a "card-carrying atheist," she surely has a significant affinity with the position advanced by Anscombe, who, as Foot puts it, "was more rigorously Catholic than the Pope."[4] After all, Foot takes Thomas Aquinas' *Summa Theologica* as "one of the best sources we have for moral philosophy," though she is quick to add that it is "as useful to the atheist as to the Catholic or other Christian believer" (VV 2). Foot's work may not have the conceptual neutrality that she claims; still, it has the virtue of a careful appreciation of the contributions of Christian moral philosophy as well as ancient Greek and contemporary analytic philosophy. This is a virtue because, as I suggested at the end of Chapter 7, we still face the challenge of sorting out which elements of traditional morality to preserve and which elements to reject. For many in North America and Europe, everyday morality is an unstable amalgam of Greek and Christian values; we compete with each other for recognition and wealth, yet, at the same time, we value humility, equality, and public service.

Of course, Foot's work does not provide an algorithm for resolving these conflicts; yet, it does more than provide a neutral philosophical framework within which the debates are to occur. It forwards a critical social vision that is shared with other moral and social philosophers such as Jürgen Habermas, John Rawls, and Tim Scanlon. At the center of this critical social vision is the idea of the individual persons as more than just "cells in a collective whole," as Warren Quinn puts it.[5] This leads Foot to endorse the general idea of morality as a contract, in which a moral code is specified and where the virtues play a limiting role (MD 76, 103). Yet, we cannot simply derive a moral code from the virtues; a rational moral code will be one that could compel conformity through a demand for reciprocity. To do so, the moral code must render benefits to each person (MD 103). This contractualist framework grows out of Foot's views about the relation of justice and charity, as outlined in Chapters 4 and 5. Great benefits to the many do not, for Foot, underwrite harm to the few; for that reason, a rational moral code will guarantee for each individual "a kind of moral space, a space which others are not *allowed* to invade" (Ibid.). And this benefit, if there is no other, provides a reason for adherence to a shared moral code.

Though Foot is far from unique in advocating these views, for most of these philosophers, they are part of a program of social reform. Rawls, for example, views his contributions to a theory of justice as part of a practical program that is, he hopes, "orienting" and "realistically utopian."[6] He hopes his philosophy will point toward, and thereby, help to bring about achievable, beneficial changes to our institutions.

It is not difficult to see how views of this sort can claim to be beneficial and reformatory. Though nearly everyone values justice and few are willing to openly advocate the idea that the individual is fungible, it is questionable whether utilitarian or other consequentialist views give adequate support for the type of restrictions on the pursuit of general welfare supported by Foot. Further, we see the maximizing conception of rationality, which she opposes, reflected in institutions driven by cost–benefit analyzes; the results of institutionalizing utilitarian thought may come at the expense of the "moral space" owed to individuals.

Foot's moral vision, then, can be characterized as a modern form of liberalism, which takes justice to be a central part of concern for the individual. Arguably, this form makes up for a blind spot in classical liberalism, which conceived of well-being in narrower terms, and was more ready to sacrifice the individual for the greater good of the whole. Foot's vision, as any vision, will seem lacking in various respects; for those sympathetic with Hare's views, it will seem to have insufficient concern with the agent's freedom to define a subjective moral conception. And despite her avowed appreciation for Thomas Aquinas, some will find that she neglected the essential role for the transcendent foundations of human purpose in his historical works. Still, this is a moral vision that must be taken seriously, for its rigorous conceptual foundations and its appreciation of the history of ethics.

NOTES

Introduction

1 In Alex Voorhoeve, *Conversations on Ethics* (Oxford: Oxford University Press, 2009), 91.

2 Of course, there were presumably factual disagreements between the Nazis and some non-Nazis inasmuch as many of the latter would presumably dissent from the racist views of the Nazis. But one could believe that there are inferior races and nevertheless not approve of genocide.

3 Ibid.

4 Peter Conradi and Gavin Lawrence, "Professor Philippa Foot: Philosopher regarded as being among the finest moral thinkers of the age" *The Independent*, October 19, 2010.

5 Voorhoeve, *Conversations*, 93.

Chapter 1

1 See, for example, A. J. Ayer, *Language, Truth and Logic* (New York: Dover, 1952), 106; C. L. Stevenson, *Ethics and Language* (New Haven: Yale University Press, 1946), 272; J. O. Urmson, *The Emotive Theory of Ethics* (London: Hutchinson & Co., 1968), 14. S. Darwall, A. Gibbard and P. Railton (eds), "Toward *Fin De Siècle* Ethics: Some Trends" in *Moral Discourse and Practice* (Oxford: Oxford University Press, 1997), 4.

2 See for example, Mary Warnock, *Ethics since 1900*, 3rd edn (Oxford: Oxford University Press, 1978), 2.

3 For a discussion of Moore's moral philosophy that focuses on the importance of this contribution, see Stephen Darwall, "How Should Ethics Relate to (the Rest of) Philosophy?: Moore's Legacy," *Southern Journal of Philosophy* 41 (2003): 1–20.

4   G. E. Moore, *Principia Ethica,* ed. Thomas Baldwin, 2nd edn (Cambridge: Cambridge University Press, 1993), 72.

5   Moore, *Principia Ethica,* 62.

6   Ibid., 59.

7   "How Should Ethics Relate to (the Rest of) Philosophy?," 12.

8   "Non-naturalism" in *Themes from G.E. Moore,* eds. Susana Nuccetelli and Gary Seay (Oxford: Oxford University Press 2007), 290ff.

9   Shaver, "Non-naturalism," 300.

10 *Language, Truth and Logic,* 107.

11 Ibid., 108.

12 C. L. Stevenson, *Ethics and Language,* 31ff.; see also *Facts and Values* (New Haven: Yale University Press, 1963), 214.

13 Stevenson, *Ethics and Language,* 33.

14 Ibid., 210.

15 Ibid., 242.

16 Ibid., 114.

17 C. L. Stevenson, "The Emotive Meaning of Ethical Terms" (1937), reprinted in *Facts and Values* (New Haven: Yale University Press, 1963), 16.

18 Ibid., 17.

19 Ludwig Wittgenstein, *Tractatus Logico-Philosophicus,* trans. D. F. Pears and B. F. McGuinness (London: Routledge & Kegan Paul, 1961), 25.

20 Whether this was, in fact, Wittgenstein's intention is unclear, and I am inclined to think that it was not his intention, at least not ultimately. Yet, this was the effect of his philosophy on a generation of philosophers, including those who developed emotivism. For a brief, but somewhat more detailed account of this sea change, see Mark Schroeder, *Noncognitivism in Ethics* (London: Routledge, 2010), 26–30. For a good summary of some of the issues involved in interpreting Wittgenstein, see Alice Crary, Introduction to *The New Wittgenstein,* eds. Alice Crary and Rupert Read (London: Routledge, 2000).

21 Stevenson, *Ethics and Language,* 118.

22 Stanley Cavell, *The Claim of Reason* (Oxford: Clarendon Press, 1979), 278.

23 Stevenson, *Ethics and Language,* 114.

24 Ibid.

25 R. M. Hare, *Objective Prescriptions, and Other Essays* (Oxford: Clarendon Press, 1999), 88.

26 R. M. Hare, *The Language of Morals* (Oxford: Oxford University Press, 1972), 13.

27 Hare, *The Language of Morals*, 28.

28 Douglas Seanor and Nicholas Fotion (eds), *Hare and Critics* (Oxford: Clarendon Press, 1988), 210.

29 Hare, *The Language of Morals*, 91.

30 Ibid., 97.

31 Ibid., 119.

32 For a late statement of this criticism, see "Objective Prescriptions," written in 1993, in *Objective Prescriptions*.

33 Hare, *Objective Prescriptions*, 8–9.

34 Hare, *The Language of Morals*, 129.

35 Ibid., 70.

36 R. M. Hare, *Freedom and Reason* (Oxford: Clarendon Press, 1963), 99.

37 Hare, *Freedom and Reason*, 116.

38 Hare, *The Language of Morals*, 181.

39 Hare, *Freedom and Reason*, 185.

40 Hare, *Objective Prescriptions*, 90.

41 Iris Murdoch, "Vision and Choice in Morality," *Proceedings of the Aristotelian Society*, sup. vol. 30 (1956): 32–58.

42 Murdoch, "Vision and Choice," 50.

43 Ibid., 47.

44 Cora Diamond, "'We are Perpetually Moralists': Iris Murdoch, Fact, and Value" in *Iris Murdoch and the Search for Human Goodness*, eds. M. Antonaccio and W. Schweiker (Chicago: University of Chicago Press, 1996), 87.

45 Murdoch, "Vision and Choice," 51.

46 Ibid., 56.

Chapter 2

1 Jeremy Bentham, *An Introduction to the Principles of Morals and Legislation*, eds. J. H. Burns and H. L. A. Hart (Oxford: Oxford University Press, 1996), 13.

2 R. M. Hare, "Descriptivism" in *Essays on the Moral Concepts* (New York: Macmillan, 1972), 71.

3 As Foot notes in VV 96; VV 111, these implications are the most significant problems in her mind for views she opposes.

4 Hare, "Descriptivism," 72.

5 An objection raised by Marvin Glass in "Philippa Foot's Naturalism: A New Version of the Breakdown Theory," *Mind*, 82 (1973): 418.

6 Anne Thomas, "Facts and Rudeness," *Mind*, 74 (1965): 399–410.

7 Glass, "Philippa Foot's Naturalism," 418. It seems possible that this view is the result of continued adherence to some of the doctrines of Stevenson and Hare at the time that she wrote "Moral Arguments," as she confesses in the 1977 introduction to *Virtues and Vices*.

8 The arguments in "Moral Beliefs" have a noticeable affinity with Wittgenstein's Private Language argument as well as his arguments about pain. See *Philosophical Investigations*, trans. G. E. M. Anscombe, P. M. S. Hacker and Joachim Schulte, 4th edn (London: Wiley-Blackwell, 2009), §243–307.

9 These examples are discussed in Justin D'Arms and Daniel Jacobson "The Significance of Recalcitrant Emotion (or, anti-quasijudgmentalism)" *Royal Institute of Philosophy Supplement* 52, 135ff.

10 See John Deigh "Cognitivism in the Theory of Emotions," *Ethics* 104 (1994): 850ff.

11 D'Arms and Jacobson, "The Significance of Recalcitrant Emotions," 129.

12 The precise connection is not spelled out in "Moral Beliefs," but in a later article "Virtues and Vices" (1977), which will be discussed in Chapter 4.

13 Obviously, there are important questions here. I will return to these points in Chapter 4, where I treat Foot's virtue ethics in greater detail.

14 She will later reject this idea in her 1972 paper, "Morality as a System of Hypothetical Imperatives," to be discussed in Chapter 3.

15 Iris Murdoch, *The Sovereignty of Good* (London: Routledge, 1970), 28.

16 See David Hume, *A Treatise of Human Nature*, eds. David Fate Norton and Mary J. Norton (Oxford: Clarendon Press, 2007), 367ff.

17 As we shall see, this claim is central to her defense of the objectivity of goodness, because for her, there is *human* goodness that is not unlike the goodness of a root, though she does not fully develop this thought until later on in *Natural Goodness*.

18 She will later, in "Morality as a System of Hypothetical Imperatives" (1972), reject the views she advocated in "Moral Beliefs" in favor of the view that we only have reason to act morally if we have certain optional desires, and she appears to believe that not everyone has the relevant desires. Later on, in "Does Moral Subjectivism Rest on a Mistake?" (1995) and in her book *Natural Goodness* (2001), she repudiates these views and returns to the belief that we all have reason to cultivate the virtues, as she advocated in "Moral Beliefs," though on quite different grounds.

19 G. E. M. Anscombe, *Intention*, 2nd edn (Cambridge, MA: Harvard University Press, 2000), 70.

20 Anscombe, *Intention*, 72ff.

21 John Rawls, *A Theory of Justice,* rev. edn (Cambridge, MA: Bellknap Press, 1999), 54.

22 Anscombe, *Intention,* 68.

23 G. E. M. Anscombe, Ethics, Religion, and Politics: Collected Papers, vol. III (Minneapolis: University of Minnesota Press), 18.

24 See Part Three of Thompson's *Life and Action* (Cambridge, MA: Harvard University Press, 2008) and LeBar's "Virtue Ethics and Deontic Constraints," *Ethics* 119 (4): 642–71. and "Aristotelian Constructivism," *Social Philosophy and Policy* 25 (1): 182–213.

25 Thompson, *Life and Action*, 167.

26 Thompson's work is unique in the literature on the subject for isolating the issue of justifying the transfer principle from the standard of appraisal, and he catches such eminent philosophers as John Rawls and T. M. Scanlon, running them together.

27 Thompson, *Life and Action*, 190.

28 Hence, it is not that the true reasons to be just must be opaque to the just agent, but rather that the agent's conception of rational action is changed.

29 See William J. Prior *"Eudaimonism* and Virtue" *The Journal of Value Inquiry* 35 (2001): 330.

Chapter 3

1 This point is brought out by Gavin Lawrence, "The Rationality of Morality," in *Virtues and Reasons*, eds. Rosalind Hursthouse, Gavin Lawrence and Warren Quinn (Oxford: Oxford University Press, 1995), 110.

2 G. E. M. Anscombe, *Intention*, 2nd edn (Cambridge, MA: Harvard University Press, 2000), 63.

3 John McDowell, "Values and Secondary Qualities," in *Mind, Value, and Reality* (Harvard, MA: Harvard University Press, 1998), 144.

4 For example, see the comparison of poems by Edgar Allen Poe and Ralph Waldo Emerson by Harold Bloom in *The Art of Reading Poetry* (New York: Harper Perennials, 2005), 25ff.

5 Indeed, she clearly later came to think so and states that she reprinted "Morality and Art" in *Moral Dilemmas* "only hesitantly" (MD 2).

6 Lawrence, "The Rationality of Morality," 109.

7 Michael Smith, *The Moral Problem* (Malden, MA: Basil Blackwell, 1994), 174.

8 Smith, *The Moral Problem*, 83.

9 Ibid., 82.

10 Sigrún Svavarsdóttir, "Moral Cogntivism and Motivation," *The Philosophical Review* 108 (1999): 161–219.

11 Svavarsdóttir, "Moral Cogntivism and Motivation," 200.

12 Ibid., 206.

13 Russ Shafer-Landau, *Moral Realism: A Defence* (Oxford: Clarendon Press, 2003), 199ff.

14 *Moral Realism*, 202.

15 Christine Korsgaard, "The Normativity of Instrumental Reason" in *Ethics and Practical Reason*, eds. G. Cullity and B. Gaut (Oxford: Oxford University Press, 1997), 223.

16 Korsgaard, "The Normativity of Instrumental Reason," 242.

17 *On What Matters*, vol. I (Oxford: Oxford University Press, 2010).

Chapter 4

1 Hence, Foot's interest in the virtues precedes Anscombe's "Modern Moral Philosophy," which is the work most often cited as initiating the revival of virtue ethics.

2 G. E. M. Anscombe, *Ethics, Religion, and Politics* (Minneapolis: University of Minnesota Press, 1981), 29.

3 Anthony Kenny, Introduction to St. Thomas Aquinas, *Summa Theologiae*, vol. 22 (New York: McGraw-Hill, 1964), xx.

4 Aquinas, Summa Theologiae, IaIIae, 49, 1, quoting Aristotle, *Metaphysics*, 1022b10–12.

5 Kenny, Introduction to St. Thomas Aquinas, xxx.

6 ST IaIIae, 50, 1.

7 See Rosalind Hursthouse, *On Virtue Ethics* (Oxford: Oxford University Press, 1999), 113–19.

8 I am here drawing on Julia Annas' distinction between "the circumstances of a life" and the "living of a life." See *Intelligent Virtue* (Oxford: Oxford University Press, 2011), 92.

9 William Prior, "*Eudaimonism* and Virtue," *The Journal of Value Inquiry* 35 (2001): 325–42.

10 Prior, "*Eudaimonism* and Virtue," 329.

11 Ibid.

12 Prior, "Eudaimonism and Virtue," 330.

13 Ibid.

14 Ibid.

15 Aquinas, *Summa Theologiae,* IaIIae 61, 3, cited at VV 9.

16 Aristotle, *Nicomachean Ethics*, trans. T. Irwin, 2nd edn (Indianapolis: Hackett Publishing, 1999), 117, VII.12 1153b17–20.

17 See *Apology* xxx. Some readers of Aristotle apparently do not find this passage dispositive on Aristotle's views on the relation between virtue and happiness. See John McDowell, "The Role of *Eudaimonia* in Aristotle's Ethics," *Essays on Aristotle's Ethics*, ed. A. Rorty (Berkeley: University of California Press, 1980), 369.

18 Perhaps her most explicit statement about this is NG 116.

19 See Justin Oakley, "Varieties of Virtue Ethics," *Ratio* 9 (1996): 129; see also Rosalind Hursthouse, *On Virtue Ethics* (Oxford: Oxford University Press, 1999), 17–25; and Christine Swanton "A Virtue Ethical Account of Right Action," *Ethics* 112 (October 2001): 32.

20 Hursthouse, *On Virtue Ethics*, 28.

21 Rosalind Hursthouse claims that Foot's statement leaves her "completely foxed" (personal communication).

22 Peter Geach, "Good and Evil," *Analysis* 17 (1956): 33–42.

23 Samuel Scheffler, *The Rejection of Consequentialism*, rev. edn (Clarendon Press: Oxford, 1994), 140.

24 Ibid.

25 Ibid., 144.

26 Philippa Foot, "For Lack of a Rationale: Review of *The Rejection of Consequentialism* by S. Scheffler," *Times Literary Supplement* 4153 (5 November 1982): 1230.

Chapter 5

1 For an overview of nonconsequentialism, see Frances Kamm, *Intricate Ethics* (Oxford: Oxford University Press, 2007), Chapter 1.

2 Presumably, there must be some number of people it would be permissible to save if it meant killing one; yet, she does not specify this number.

3 Warren Quinn, *Morality and Action* (Cambridge: Cambridge University Press, 1994), 171.

4 Ibid.

5 See John Taurek, "Should the Numbers Count?" *Philosophy and Public Affairs* 6 (1977): 293–316.

6 Frances Kamm points out a lacuna in both Foot and Quinn's account of the rationale for the precedence of negative rights. In order to achieve the kind of integrity that Foot and Quinn seem agreed in viewing as a basis for the DDA, we need not only negative rights, but also prerogatives. Prerogatives allow us to pursue projects that we have committed to, even when we could redistribute our efforts to greater advantage. Unless we have such prerogatives, positive rights make demands on us that would prevent us from having control over the direction of our efforts, which is clearly something that the rationale advanced by Foot and Quinn requires. Although prerogatives are compatible with the views that Foot embraces, Foot does not discuss them. See Kamm, *Intricate Ethics*, 82.

7 Quinn, *Morality and Action*, 159.

8 Ibid., 160.

9 Jonathan Bennett, *The Act Itself* (New York: Oxford University Press, 1995), 210.

10 Quinn, *Morality and Action*, 185.

11 For criticisms of this proposal, see John Martin Fischer, Mark Ravizza, and David Copp, "Quinn on Double Effect: The Problem of Closeness," *Ethics* 103 (July 1993): 707–25.

12 Judith Jarvis Thomson, "Physician-Assisted Suicide: Two Moral Arguments," *Ethics* 109 (April 1999): 515–16.

13 T. M. Scanlon, *Moral Dimensions* (Cambridge, MA: Bellknap Press, 2008), 19–20.

14 G. E. M. Anscombe, *Intention,* 2nd edn (Cambridge, MA: Harvard University Press, 2000), 8.

15 Quinn, *Morality and Action*, 190.

16 Judith Jarvis Thomson, "The Trolley Problem," *The Yale Law Journal* 94, 6 (May 1985): 1397.

17 Thomson, "The Trolley Problem," 1412.

18 Kamm, *Intricate Ethics*, 96.

19 Ibid.

20 Quinn, *Morality and Action*, 150.

21 Judith Jarvis Thomson, "A Defense of Abortion," *Philosophy and Public Affairs*, 1 (Fall 1971): 48.

22 Rosalind Hursthouse, "Virtue Theory and Abortion," *Philosophy and Public Affairs*, 20 (Summer 1991): 223–46.

23 John Hacker-Wright, "Moral Status in Virtue Ethics," *Philosophy*, 82 (2007): 449–73.

24 James Rachels, "Active and Passive Euthanasia," *New England Journal of Medicine* 292 (9 January 1975): 78–80.

Chapter 6

1 Portions of this chapter were published previously; see "What Is Natural About Foot's Ethical Naturalism?" *Ratio* 22, no. 3 (2009): 308–21; see also Ethical Naturalism and the Constitution of Agency," *Journal of Value Inquiry* 46, no. 1 (2012): 13–23; and "Human Nature, Virtue, and Rationality" in *Aristotelian Ethics in Contemporary Perspective*, ed. Julia Peters (London: Routledge, 2012).

2 See *Dying We Live*, eds. H. Gollwitzer, K. Kuhn and R. Schneider (London: The Harvill Press, 1956).

3 Warren Quinn, *Morality and Action* (Cambridge: Cambridge University Press, 1994), 216.

4 Michael Thompson, *Life and Action* (Cambridge, MA: Harvard University Press, 2008), 56.

5 Thompson, *Life and Action*, 57.

6 Michael Thompson, "Three Degrees of Natural Goodness" originally in Italian in *Iride*, 2003, English text at http://www.pitt.edu/%7emthompso/three.pdf (last accessed March 25, 2008).

7 Thompson, *Life and Action*, 43.

8 Chrisoula Andreou, "Getting On in a Varied World," *Social Theory and Practice* 32 (2006): 61–73.

9 Joseph Millum, "Natural Goodness and Natural Evil," *Ratio* 19 (2006): 199–213.

10 Millum, "Natural Goodness and Natural Evil," 205.

11 A more detailed treatment of the objections arising from evolutionary biology can be found in Micah Lott, "Have Elephant Seals Refuted Aristotle? Nature, Function, and Moral Goodness," *Journal of Moral Philosophy* 9 (2012): 353–75.

12 Millum, "Natural Goodness and Natural Evil," 205.

13 Scott Woodcock, "Philippa Foot's Virtue Ethics Has an Achilles' Heel," *Dialogue* 45 (2006): 445–68.

14 Woodcock, "Philippa Foot's Virtue Ethics," 452.

15 Robert Crouch, "Letting the Deaf Be Deaf: Reconsidering the Use of Cochlear Implants in Prelingually Deaf Children," *The Hastings Center Report* 27 (July–August 1997): 14–21.

16 See "Two Sorts of Naturalism" in *Mind, Value, and Reality* (Cambridge, MA: Harvard University Press, 1998).

17 Thompson, "Three Degrees of Natural Goodness," n.p.

18 G. E. M. Anscombe, *Intention*, 2nd edn (Cambridge, MA: Harvard University Press, 2000), 49.

19 "Apprehending Human Form," in *Modern Moral Philosophy*, ed. Anthony O'Hear (Cambridge: Cambridge University Press, 2004), 69.

Chapter 7

1 Thomas Mann, *Nietzsche's Philosophy in the Light of Recent Events* (Washington, DC: Library of Congress, 1947), 35.

2 Friedrich Nietzsche, *The Anti-Christ, Ecce Homo, Twilight of the Idols and Other Writings*, eds. Aaron Ridley and Judith Norman, trans. Judith Norman (Cambridge: Cambridge University Press, 2005), 148.

3 Friedrich Nietzsche, *Daybreak*, eds. Maudemarie Clark and Brian Leiter, trans. R. J. Hollingdale (Cambridge: Cambridge University Press, 1997), 60.

4 Ibid.

5 Maudemarie Clark, Introduction to *On the Genealogy of Morality* by Friedrich Nietzsche, eds. and trans. Maudemarie Clark and Alan J. Swensen (Indianapolis: Hackett Press, 2006), xviii.

6 Hereafter, when I refer to "morality," I mean morality in the narrow sense, specifically, Western morality.

7   See Michael Tanner, *Nietzsche* (Oxford: Oxford University Press, 1994), 34.

8   Nietzsche, *On the Genealogy of Morality*, 10.

9   Ibid., 57.

10 Cf. Jesse Prinz, "Against Empathy," *The Southern Journal of Philosophy* 49 (2011): 214–33.

11 Nietzsche, *Daybreak*, 90.

12 Ibid., 84 (translation modified).

13 For evidence that Nietzsche is wrong about the motives of human beings, see C. Daniel Batson, *Altruism in Humans* (Oxford: Oxford University Press, 2011).

14 Nietzsche, *Daybreak*, 85.

15 Ibid., 87. See also Friedrich Nietzsche, *Beyond Good and Evil*, eds. Rolf-Peter Horstmann and Judith Norman, trans. Judith Norman (Cambridge: Cambridge University Press, 2002), 31.

16 Nietzsche, *Beyond Good and Evil*, 116.

17 Friedrich Nietzsche, *The Gay Science,* ed. Bernard Williams, trans. Josefine Nauckhoff (Cambridge: Cambridge University Press, 2001), 192.

18 Ibid., 191.

19 Nietzsche, *Beyond Good and Evil*, 116.

20 Nietzsche, *The Gay Science*, 192.

21 For evidence that Nietzsche is wrong about the motives of human beings, see C. Daniel Batson, *Altruism in Humans* (Oxford: Oxford University Press, 2011).

22 François de La Rochefoucauld, *Collected Maxims and Other Reflections*, trans. E. H. and A. M. Blackmore and Francine Giguère (Oxford: Oxford University Press, 2008), 3.

23 See Chapter 6.

24 Nietzsche, *On the Genealogy of Morality*, 50.

25 Ibid., 22.

26 See Chapter 6 for further elaboration of Foot's position.

27 See Maudemarie Clarke, "Nietzsche's Immoralism and the Concept of Morality" in *Nietzsche, Genealogy, Morality*, ed. Richard Schacht (Berkeley: University of California Press, 1994); see also Mark Migotti, "Slave Morality, Socrates, and the Bushmen: A Reading of the First Essay of *On the Genealogy of Morals*," *Philosophy and Phenomenological Research* 58, no. 4 (1998): 745–79.

28   Nietzsche, *On the Genealogy of Morality*, 23.

29   Friedrich Nietzsche, *Thus Spoke Zarathustra*, eds. Adrian Del Caro and Robert Pippin, trans. Adrian Del Caro (Cambridge: Cambridge University Press, 2006), 155.

30   Nietzsche, *On the Genealogy of Morality*, 50.

31   Ibid., 33.

Chapter 8

1   Wittgenstein, *Philosophical Investigations*, trans. G. E. M. Anscombe, P. M. S. Hacker and Joachim Schulte, 4th edn (London: Wiley-Blackwell, 2009), §124, 55.

2   Wittgenstein, *Philosophical Investigations*, §115, 53.

3   Murdoch, "Vision and Choice," *Proceedings of the Aristotelian Society,* sup. vol. 30 (1956): 47.

4   Voorhoeve, *Conversations on Ethics*, *Conversations on Ethics* (Oxford: Oxford University Press, 2009), 93.

5   Quinn, *Morality and Action*, *Morality and Action* (Cambridge: Cambridge University Press, 1994), 171.

6   Rawls, *Justice as Fairness*, ed. Erin Kelly (Cambridge, MA: Belknap Press of Harvard University Press, 2001), 4.

WORKS CITED

Andreou, Chrisoula. "Getting On in a Varied World." *Social Theory and Practice* 32, no. 1 (2006): 61–73.

Annas, Julia. *Intelligent Virtue*. Oxford: Oxford University Press, 2011.

Anscombe, G. E. M. *Ethics, Religion, and Politics*. Minneapolis: University of Minnesota Press, 1981.

—. *Intention*, 2nd edn. Cambridge, MA: Harvard University Press, 2000.

Antonaccio, Maria, and William Schweiker, eds. *Iris Murdoch and the Search for Human Goodness*. Chicago: University of Chicago Press, 1996.

Aquinas, St Thomas, *St. Thomas Aquinas: Summa Theologiae: Volume 22 (1a2ae. 49–54), Dispositions for Human Acts*. Edited by Anthony Kenny. New York: McGraw-Hill, 1964.

Aristotle. *Nicomachean Ethics*. Translated by Terence Irwin, 2nd edn. Indianapolis: Hackett Publishing, 1999.

Ayer, A. J. *Language, Truth and Logic*. New York: Dover Publications, 1952.

Batson, C. Daniel. *Altruism in Humans*. Oxford: Oxford University Press, 2011.

Bennett, Jonathan. *The Act Itself*. Oxford: Oxford University Press, 1998.

Bentham, Jeremy. *An Introduction to the Principles of Morals and Legislation*. Edited by J. H. Burns and H. L. A. Hart. Oxford: Oxford University Press, 1996.

Bloom, Harold. *The Art of Reading Poetry*. New York: Harper Perennial, 2005.

Cavell, Stanley. *The Claim of Reason: Wittgenstein, Skepticism, Morality, and Tragedy*. Oxford: Oxford University Press, 1979.

Crary, Alice, and Rupert J. Read. *The New Wittgenstein*. London: Routledge, 2000.

Crouch, R. A. "Letting the Deaf Be Deaf: Reconsidering the Use of Cochlear Implants in Prelingually Deaf Children." *Hastings Center Report* 27, no. 4 (1997): 14–21.

Cullity, Garrett, and Berys Gaut, eds. *Ethics and Practical Reason*. Oxford: Oxford University Press, 1998.

D'Arms, Justin, and Daniel Jacobson. "The Significance of Recalcitrant Emotion (or, Anti-quasijudgmentalism)." *Philosophy and the Emotions: Royal Institute of Philosophy Supplements* 52 (2003): 127–45.

Darwall, Stephen. "How Should Ethics Relate to (the Rest of) Philosophy?: Moore's Legacy." *The Southern Journal of Philosophy* 41, Supplement (2003): 1–20.

Darwall, Stephen, Allan Gibbard, and Peter Railton, eds. *Moral Discourse and Practice: Some Philosophical Approaches*. Oxford: Oxford University Press, 1999.

Deigh, J. "Cognitivism in the Theory of Emotions." *Ethics* 104, no. 4 (1994): 824–54.

Fischer, John Martin, Mark Ravizza, and David Copp. "Quinn on Double Effect: The Problem of 'Closeness'." *Ethics* 103, no. 4 (1993): 707–25.

Foot, Philippa. *Moral Dilemmas and Other Topics in Moral Philosophy*. Oxford: Oxford University Press, 2002.

—. *Natural Goodness*. Oxford: Oxford University Press, 2001.

—. "The Philosopher's Defence of Morality." *Philosophy* 27, no. 103 (1952): 311–28.

—. *Virtues and Vices and Other Essays in Moral Philosophy*, 2nd edn. Oxford: Oxford University Press, 2002.

—. "When Is a Principle a Moral Principle?" *Aristotelian Society Supplementary Volume* 28 (1954): 95–110.

—, ed. *Theories of Ethics*. Oxford: Oxford University Press, 1976.

Geach, P. T. "Good and Evil." *Analysis* 17, no. 2 (1956): 33–42.

Glass, Marvin. "Philippa Foot's Naturalism: A New Version of the Breakdown Theory of Ethics." *Mind* 82, no. 327 (1973): 417–20.

Gollwitzer, Helmut, Kathe Kuhn, and Reinhold Schneider, eds. *Dying We Live: The Final Messages and Records of the Resistance*. Eugene, OR: Wipf & Stock Publishers, 2005.

Hacker-Wright, John. "Ethical Naturalism and the Constitution of Agency." *Journal of Value Inquiry* 46, no. 1 (2012): 13–23.

—. "Human Nature, Personhood, and Ethical Naturalism." *Philosophy* 84, no. 3 (2009): 413–27.

—. "Moral Status in Virtue Ethics." *Philosophy* 82, no. 3 (2007): 449–73.

—. "What Is Natural About Foot's Ethical Naturalism?" *Ratio* 22, no. 3 (2009): 308–21.

Hare, R. M. *Essays on the Moral Concepts*. Berkeley: University of California Press, 1972.

—. *Freedom and Reason*. Oxford: Clarendon Press, 1963.

—. *Moral Thinking: Its Levels, Method, and Point*. Oxford: Clarendon Press Oxford, 1981.

—. *Objective Prescriptions and Other Essays*. Oxford: Clarendon Press, 1999.

—. *The Language of Morals*. Oxford: Clarendon Press, 1952.

Hume, David. *A Treatise of Human Nature*. Edited by David Fate Norton and Mary Norton. Oxford: Oxford: Clarendon Press, 2000.

Hursthouse, Rosalind. *On Virtue Ethics*. Oxford: Oxford University Press, 1999.

—. "Virtue Theory and Abortion." *Philosophy and Public Affairs* 20, no. 3 (1991): 223–46.

Hursthouse, Rosalind, Gavin Lawrence, and Warren Quinn, eds. *Virtues and Reasons: Philippa Foot and Moral Theory: Essays in Honour of Philippa Foot*. Oxford: Oxford University Press, 1995.

Kamm, F. M. *Intricate Ethics: Rights, Responsibilities, and Permissible Harm*. Oxford: Oxford University Press, 2007.

LeBar, Mark. "Aristotelian Constructivism." *Social Philosophy and Policy* 25, no. 1 (2008): 182–213.

—. "Virtue Ethics and Deontic Constraints." *Ethics* 119, no. 4 (2009): 642–71.

Lott, Micah. "Have Elephant Seals Refuted Aristotle? Nature, Function, and Moral Goodness." *Journal of Moral Philosophy* 9, no. 3 (2012): 353–75.

Mann, Thomas. *Nietzsche's Philosophy in the Light of Contemporary Events*. Washington: The Library of Congress, 1947.

McDowell, John. *Mind, Value, and Reality*. Cambridge, MA: Harvard University Press, 2001.

Migotti, Mark. "Slave Morality, Socrates, and the Bushmen: A Reading of the First Essay of on the Genealogy of Morals." *Philosophy and Phenomenological Research* 58, no. 4 (1998): 745–79.

Millum, Joseph. "Natural Goodness and Natural Evil." *Ratio* 19, no. 2 (2006): 199–213.

Moore, G. E. *Principia Ethica*. Edited by Thomas Baldwin, 2nd edn. Cambridge: Cambridge University Press, 1993.

Murdoch, Iris. *The Sovereignty of the Good*. London: Routledge, 1970.

—. "Vision and Choice in Morality." *Proceedings of the Aristotelian Society*, Supplement 30 (1956): 14–58.

Nietzsche, Friedrich. *Daybreak: Thoughts on the Prejudices of Morality*. Edited by Maudemarie Clark and Brian Leiter, 2nd edn. Cambridge: Cambridge University Press, 1997.

—. *Beyond Good and Evil: Prelude to a Philosophy of the Future*. Edited by Rolf-Peter Horstmann. Translated by Judith Norman. Cambridge: Cambridge University Press, 2001.

—. *On the Genealogy of Morality*. Edited by Maudemarie Clark. Translated by Alan J. Swensen. Indianapolis: Hackett Publishing, 1998.

—. *The Anti-Christ, Ecce Homo, Twilight of the Idols: And Other Writings*. Edited by Aaron Ridley. Translated by Judith Norman. Cambridge: Cambridge University Press, 2005.

—. *The Gay Science: With a Prelude in German Rhymes and an Appendix of Songs*. Edited by Bernard Williams. Translated by Josefine Nauckhoff and Adrian Del Caro. Cambridge: Cambridge University Press, 2001.

—. *Thus Spoke Zarathustra*. Edited by Robert Pippin. Translated by
   Adrian Del Caro. Cambridge: Cambridge University Press, 2006.

Nuccetelli, Susana, and Gary Seay, eds. *Themes from G. E. Moore:
   New Essays in Epistemology and Ethics*. Oxford: Oxford University
   Press, 2008.

O'Hear, Anthony, ed. *Modern Moral Philosophy: Royal Institute of
   Philosophy Supplement 54*. Cambridge: Cambridge University Press,
   2004.

Oakley, Justin. "Varieties of Virtue Ethics." *Ratio* 9, no. 2 (1996): 128–52.

Parfit, Derek. *On What Matters, Vol. 1*. Oxford: Oxford University Press,
   2011.

Peters, Julia, ed. *Aristotelian Ethics in Contemporary Perspective*. London:
   Routledge, 2012.

Prinz, Jesse. "Against Empathy." *Southern Journal of Philosophy* 49, no.
   s1 (2011): 214–33.

Prior, William J. "Eudaimonism and Virtue." *Journal of Value Inquiry* 35,
   no. 3 (2001): 325–42.

Quinn, Warren. *Morality and Action*. Cambridge: Cambridge University
   Press, 1994.

Rachels, J. "Active and Passive Euthanasia." *New England Journal of
   Medicine* 292, no. 2 (1975): 78–80.

Rawls, John. *A Theory of Justice*, rev. edn. Cambridge, MA: Harvard
   University Press, 1999.

—. *Justice as Fairness: A Restatement*. Edited by Erin Kelly. Cambridge,
   MA: Belknap Press of Harvard University Press, 2001.

Rochefoucauld, Francois de La. *Collected Maxims and Other Reflections*.
   Translated by E. H. Blackmore, A. M. Blackmore and Francine
   Giguère. Oxford: Oxford University Press, 2008.

Rorty, Amélie Oksenberg, ed. *Essays on Aristotle's Ethics*. Eight
   Impression. University of California Press, 1981.

Scanlon, T. M. *Moral Dimensions: Permissibility, Meaning, Blame*.
   Cambridge, MA: Belknap Press of Harvard University Press, 2010.

Schacht, Richard, ed. *Nietzsche, Genealogy, Morality: Essays on
   Nietzsche's On the Genealogy of Morals*. Berkeley: University of
   California Press, 1994.

Scheffler, Samuel. *The Rejection of Consequentialism: A Philosophical
   Investigation of the Considerations Underlying Rival Moral
   Conceptions*, rev. edn. Oxford: Oxford University Press, 1994.

Schroeder, Mark. *Noncognitivism in Ethics*. London; New York:
   Routledge, 2010.

Seanor, Douglas, and Fotion, Nicholas, eds. *Hare and Critics: Essays on
   Moral Thinking*. Oxford: Clarendon Press, 1988.

Shafer-Landau, Russ. *Moral Realism: A Defence*. Oxford: Oxford
   University Press, 2005.

Smith, Michael. *The Moral Problem*, 1st edn. Malden, MA: Wiley-Blackwell, 1994.

Stevenson, C. L. *Ethics and Language*. New Haven: Yale University Press, 1944.

—. *Facts and Values*. New Haven: Yale University Press, 1963.

Svavarsdóttir, Sigrun. "Moral Cognitivism and Motivation." *The Philosophical Review* 108, no. 2 (April 1999): 161. doi:10.2307/2998300.

Swanton, Christine. "A Virtue Ethical Account of Right Action." *Ethics* 112, no. 1 (2001): 32–52.

Tanner, Michael. *Nietzsche*. Oxford: Oxford University Press, 1994.

Taurek, John M. "Should the Numbers Count?" *Philosophy and Public Affairs* 6, no. 4 (1977): 293–316.

Thomas, Anne Lloyd. "Facts and Rudeness." *Mind* 74, no. 295 (1965): 399–410.

Thompson, Michael. *Life and Action: Elementary Structures of Practice and Practical Thought*. Cambridge, MA: Harvard University Press, 2012.

—. "Three Degrees of Natural Goodness (Discussion note, Iride)." *Iride* (manuscript). http://www.pitt.edu/~mthompso/three.pdf.

Thomson, Judith Jarvis. "A Defense of Abortion." *Philosophy and Public Affairs* 1, no. 1 (1971): 47–66.

—. "Physician Assisted Suicide: Two Moral Arguments." *Ethics* 109, no. 3 (1999): 497–518.

—. "The Trolley Problem." *Yale Law Journal* 94 (1985): 1395–415.

Urmson, J. O. *The Emotive Theory of Ethics*. London: Hutchinson London, 1968.

Voorhoeve, Alex. *Conversations on Ethics*. Oxford: Oxford University Press, 2009.

Warnock, Mary. *Ethics Since 1900*, 3rd edn. Oxford: Oxford University Press, 1978.

Wittgenstein, Ludwig. *Philosophical Investigations*. Edited by P. M. S. Hacker and Joachim Schulte, 4th edn. New York: Wiley-Blackwell, 2009.

—. *Tractatus Logico-Philosophicus*. Translated by D. F. Pears and B. F. McGuiness. London: Routledge, 1961.

Woodcock, Scott. "Philippa Foot's Virtue Ethics Has an Achilles' Heel." *Dialogue* 45, no. 3 (2006): 445–68.

INDEX